SANDRA POST AND ME

SANDRA POST AND ME

A Veteran Pro Takes a New Golfer
from First Swing to Tournament

SANDRA POST and LORAL DEAN

M&S

Canadian Cataloguing in Publication Data

Post, Sandra, 1948–
    Sandra Post and me: a veteran pro takes a new golfer from first swing to tournament

Includes index.

ISBN 0-7710-7041-1

1. Golf for women. I. Dean, Loral. II. Title.

GV966.P67 1998   796.352'082   C97-932714-8

We acknowledge the financial support of the Government of Canada through the Book Publishing Industry Development Program for our publishing activities. We further acknowledge the support of the Canada Council for the Arts and the Ontario Arts Council for our publishing program.

Book design by Sari Ginsberg
Illustrations by Pam Davies
Photographs by Don Vickery

Set in Goudy Old Style by M&S, Toronto
Printed and bound in Canada

McClelland & Stewart Inc.
The Canadian Publishers
481 University Avenue
Toronto, Ontario
M5G 2E9

1 2 3 4 5   02 01 00 99 98

This book is dedicated to my father, Clifford Secord Post, who introduced me to the game of golf, was my first golf teacher, and, to this day, is my most avid supporter. Also, to my mother, Muriel Nixon Post, who never played the game, but did all the little things and gave me unconditional encouragement throughout my entire life.
– S.P.

For David, love of my life
– L.D.

CONTENTS

PART III: FROM FIRST SWING TO TOURNAMENT
IN A SINGLE SEASON

ACKNOWLEDGEMENTS

My thanks to:

The Honourable John H. McDermid: My husband. Thanks to your inspiration and encouragement, I'll tackle almost any project. We grow together.

Elmer Priestkorn: PGA teaching professional and my teacher. Taught LPGA players over five decades. He never told me I was talented until I retired. That was his strength; he knew his players.

Marilynn Smith: Founding member of the LPGA and twenty-two-time winner on tour. Marilynn befriended me in 1953 when I was five years old. If she hadn't spoken to me, given me a glove, ball, and tees, then become my pen pal, who knows? One of the great ambassadors for golf.

Marlene Stewart-Streit: The most successful amateur golfer Canada has ever produced. Thank you for setting a winning example. Your determination and competitiveness elevated women's amateur golf internationally.

Kathy Whitworth: LPGA Hall of Fame member, winner of eighty-eight tour events. Thank you for encouraging me when I first played an exhibition match with you when I was fourteen, for your great advice along the way, for being such a gracious person, humble but such a pillar.

Sybil Griffin: Former LPGA player and teacher. For generously giving of your spare time in the winter months, helping me with my game.

Susie Berning: LPGA Tour player with eleven wins, including three U.S. Open championships. Thank you for befriending me early in my professional career. You speak your mind and have little fear. What an inspiration.

Renée Powell: LPGA member. Renée and her family are the only African-American family in the United States who have built, and own and operate their own golf course, Clearview Golf Course in East Canton, Ohio. Renée's life and mine parallel one another in many ways. We competed against each other in amateur golf, were roommates my first year on tour, and remain friends, comparing notes weekly to this day. Renée's dignity and grace are an inspiration. We share common beliefs and continue to support each other.

Bob Rosburg: Former PGA Tour player and tour winner. Currently a broadcaster with ABC Sports. Thank you for sharing a little of your golf knowledge. What a guru of golf. Your putting lesson during the 1979 Dinah Shore made my winning that tournament possible.

Larry Armitage: Manager of the Family Golf Centre in Oakville, Ontario. Thank you for suggesting I teach golf, and for giving me a facility in which to begin.

Harold and Angelica Meyers: Owners of the Oakville Executive Golf Course, Oakville, Ontario. Thank you for being friends first and assisting me in developing the short-game clinics at your course. We are a good team.

Judy and "Yippy" Walter Rankin: Judy is a former LPGA Tour player, winner of twenty-two tour events, and currently a broadcaster for ABC Sports. Thank you both for a long and loyal friendship. You were the best at golf-course management, and I tried to learn as much as I could from your experience. What a team!

Marlene Hagge: Thank you for a long friendship. Your shared knowledge about the game, equipment, and courses was invaluable, and your great stories, especially about the "Babe" (Babe Zaharias), were always entertaining.

My students: From new golfer to club champion to tour player, you are all my inspirations, for we share the love of golf.

Loral Dean: Author! Golfer! Thank you for accepting the challenge.

– Sandra Post

The only thing I had to do with the idea that created this book was be in the right place at the right time. First tee-off came from Sandra, fuelled by her enthusiasm – and frustration. She knew there wasn't a single book out there she could refer her students to that spoke directly to what she knew they would have to go through when they tackled the game of golf. The next ball, off the fairway, was hit by my husband, David Cobb. He suggested it be a real-life story about Sandra Post, seasoned pro, teaching Loral Dean, raw beginner, the basics. Veteran journalist and golfer Ken Becker hit the next ball pin high when he came up with a workable story outline. Start on the practice tee, progress to the golf course, and build to a climax in a golf tournament, he counselled. Karen O'Reilly, Sandra's and my brilliant agent, holed out when she transformed this fledgling idea into a dazzling marketing-cum-book proposal no sane publisher could resist. All I did from tee-off time on was try to keep up with everyone else's suggestions, and scribble down a few notes.

I never would have swung a golf club if it hadn't been for Dianne Jackson. Dianne remains my first golf mentor, as well as a dear friend. In addition to Sandra's (and her husband, John McDermid's) tireless instruction, three golf pros have given me invaluable tips, and I thank them. They are Helen Smith of Wilmington, North Carolina, and Jill Fraser and Gary Price of the Sandra Post School of Golf.

My kindred spirit Sara Wolch, who knew (and cared) even less about golf than I did when I began this book, believed in the project from the start and remained steadfast throughout my purgatory. This was an act of blind faith approaching the heroic, and it came from a true friend.

From my stumbling beginnings at golf and throughout the writing of this book, Andy Donato, a passionate devotee of the game, has been generous with his expertise as an artist and a student of the game.

The splendid photographs inside and out are the work of longtime golf photographer (and jazz musician) Don Vickery, a true pro and a pleasure to work with. The numerous illustrations within that accompany Sandra's step-by-step instruction are the outstanding achievement of Pam Davies, an accomplished artist.

Working with the truly professional team at McClelland & Stewart has been a pleasure and a privilege for Sandra and me. Our editor, Pat Kennedy, is an editing pro par excellence. When she tackled this manuscript, the world of golf was as strange and unknown to her as it had been to me. But she guided Sandra and me through the minefield of golf minutiae, pointing out inconsistencies and even technical errors with amazing accuracy. Sandra and I will continue our (so far fruitless) attempts to persuade her to take up the game herself, armed with her newly acquired expertise.

Heather Sangster, also a golf neophyte and consummate professional, completed the editorial team. She saved us from ourselves many times, proving once again that golf is in the details.

The design challenge that this book presented, with its imponderable mix of two writers' voices – and numerous sidebars, illustrations, photographs, and cutlines – was at least equal to the challenge of taking up golf at age fifty-three. Sari Ginsberg, yet another golf neophyte (and nowhere close to fifty-three), is responsible for the beautiful-looking book you are holding.

There are at least two accomplished golfers at McClelland & Stewart, president and owner Avie Bennett and publisher Douglas Gibson, whose room-in-residence at St. Andrew's University in Scotland overlooked the legendary 17th fairway of the Royal and Ancient golf course. Sandra and I thank them both for their keen interest in this book, as well as their hands-on commitment to it. And Marilyn Luce's welcoming face and empathetic smile, which greets all who disembark from the elevators on the ninth floor of 481 University Avenue, epitomizes the guiding spirit behind "The Canadian Publishers."

– Loral Dean

PROLOGUE

SANDRA SPEAKS:
WELCOME TO MY WORLD OF GOLF

I fell in love with golf at the age of five thanks to my dad, who was a top-notch amateur golfer. Golf came naturally to me and I loved the game right from the start. I've never looked back. I turned pro when I was nineteen and won the Ladies Professional Golf Association (LPGA) championship six months later against the legendary Kathy Whitworth. It was June 1968 and I'd just celebrated my twentieth birthday. I spent sixteen extraordinary years on the road with the Tour, won nine tournaments, and came second in twenty more. I travelled the world, met more movie stars and heads of state than I can count, and had the time of my young life. But, as the saying goes, that's another story. In the fourteen years since I left the Tour and decided to return to my beloved Canada, I have built a professional life that includes teaching, broadcasting, public speaking, and, in 1997, editing a new magazine for women golfers, *World of Women's Golf*, and playing in the new women's Medalist Tour for LPGA pros over the age of forty.

I enjoy it all – but then I enjoy anything remotely connected to the game of golf! I can also say, without question, that my students are the greatest single joy of my professional life.

Every year, I teach hundreds of golfers at my School of Golf, which has locations in both Caledon and Oakville, Ontario. Every year, 347,000 people in Canada take up golf, and 52 per cent of them are women. (In the United States every year, two million people take up golf.) This exciting trend in women's golf is reflected at my school: about 70 per cent of my students are women. Some, particularly busy career women, choose private lessons. But the vast majority sign up for one of my golf clinics – three one-and-one-quarter-hour classes on three consecutive days, with five students in each group. Women enjoy the companionship of other women who are learning the same skills, and they learn a lot from one another in small groups.

I chose Loral Dean as my representative student for this book because she fits the profile of so many of my beginner students. You could almost call her a composite (although I find it hard to label her this way after getting to know her so well over the past one hundred days!). But in outline, this is Loral, a typical woman newcomer to the game of golf: She's in her early fifties. She's reasonably fit, but she's not really athletic. She's lived a pressure-cooker life for most of her adult years, combining marriage, children, and career. Now her children have grown up and left home and her husband is close to retirement. And he loves to play golf. For the first time in many years, Loral feels she can clear a few hours in her busy schedule just for herself – and for golf.

Not that all my women students are middle-aged. As more women move into management positions, many are taking up golf for the same business reasons so many men have for generations. I teach lots of driven, Type-A career women in their twenties and thirties. And I also teach women in their twenties, thirties, and forties who are trying to do it all, and all at once – career, marriage, family, *and* golf. Many of these women learn the basics, then put golf on the back burner for a few years because of the many demands of their busy lives.

Of course, in an ideal world, everyone would take up golf as a child, the way I did, when your body is like a rubber band. But not everyone is as fortunate as I was. Golf often comes easier for young women, as Loral discovered with a tinge of envy. The human body is more flexible and forgiving when you're under fifty, and often, at least at the beginning, progress seems a lot faster. But no matter what your age or personal circumstances when you take up the game, the journey from raw beginner to proficient golfer is the same for everyone. I watch hundreds of my students of all ages go through the same roller coaster of emotions and series of successes and failures that Loral has experienced this summer.

I cannot overemphasize the importance of starting golf with a solid grounding in the basics. No matter what your goal – simply enjoying a few hours with friends in a green setting or becoming a low handicapper or scratch golfer – you will never enjoy or appreciate the game the way it deserves if you don't first learn the basics – grip, stance, posture, and alignment – and the essential parts of the golf swing. At the same time, you must also learn a few of the important rules and points of etiquette of this ancient game. It deserves nothing less.

Once you've learned the basics, you can work on your swing and your short-game skills (pitching, chipping, putting) for as long as you choose to play. Golf is a game in which you never stop learning, and I include myself and every pro on the PGA and LPGA Tours in this.

It's true that Loral was a special student this summer. I certainly saw a lot of her. But I did not treat her specially (I believe she has some gripes about this in her story!). In fact, I didn't give her a single private lesson during her entire hundred days of golf. And I went out of my way not to single her out when she participated in my group clinics, although I do make a special effort in my clinics to teach each student as an individual. Every student is different, and everyone learns in his or her own way. I keep my classes small for this reason: I want every student to leave with a sense of accomplishment and improvement, and I can only achieve this by focusing on each person individually.

I did give Loral unlimited access to my School of Golf's practice facilities. And she practised often, by herself, the way all golfers must learn to do if they want to improve. We played a few holes of golf together on a short, or "executive," course, the kind of course that suits a beginner. But the only eighteen holes we have played together – on a very long course, much too long for a beginner – was the corporate tournament I threw her into to cap her hundred-day intensive introduction to the game. I won't spoil Loral's story by telling how she performed in the tournament, but I will say that, as the countdown to the tournament approached, she reverted to the same bundle of nerves I met at her first lesson!

I love introducing people to this wonderful game – and to the world it opens up. Because golf does open up a whole new life. You must trust me on this. Golf can change your life for the better and for the best, forever.

I *know* this and I also know that, given a little time and opportunity, I can convey this to every one of my students. I love being there when that magical moment happens. Sometimes it's when they hit the ball with that satisfying *ping* and see it soar into the air for the first time. Sometimes the moment it happens is on a golf course when they experience the beauty and peace of the surroundings. Sometimes, for students who have played the game without much enthusiasm (or with simple terror) in business situations, it happens when they suddenly "get" it and realize the joy of unlocking the treasures the game has to offer.

Even though we usually play golf with other people, in the end golf is a solitary game. Unlike other sports in which we react to shots from an opponent, in golf we must play every ball alone. Loral learned this, as every student of the game must. She spent many hours practising by herself both at my School of Golf practice range and at public ranges far from my critical eye. This was as it should have been. I knew that if I stood over Loral, the game would never become her own. I wanted her to discover the riches golf has to offer for *Loral* – not for me, not for her husband, David, and certainly not for this book.

LORAL SPEAKS:
MY HUNDRED-DAY JOURNEY INTO GOLF

For the past hundred days, golf has been at the centre of my life. I started my journey into the heart of golf as a raw beginner, and, a hundred days later, I've come out the other end . . . a seasoned beginner! Yes, I've learned an enormous amount, thanks in no small part to Sandra's enthusiasm, encouragement, and expertise. But my real achievement – and it is not a small one – is my appreciation of how little I know about this ancient game, and of how much there is to learn.

Over one hundred days and nights, I've learned the basics, I've practised, and I've played, sweated, discussed, talked, watched, walked, read, written, eaten, drunk, and dreamt golf. During this intense initiation into a world formerly alien to me, I've experienced pretty well everything the game can offer – joy and despair, pride and humiliation, elation and depression, smug superiority and painful envy, simple pleasure, peace, companionship, solitude, boundless energy and acute fatigue, aching muscles, sore feet, blisters, mosquito bites, dehydration, sunburn, gale-force winds, rain, freezing temperatures, debilitating heat, muggy, polluted air, clean, country air, rudeness and kindness, patience, impatience, frustration, delight. The full golf gamut.

You may already have begun your own golf journey – or you may be debating whether to embark. In either case, if you embrace the game, a thousand obstacles will arise between you and the single-minded pursuit of a perfect golf swing. Work, family responsibilities, other interests will get in the way. If you're like me and are not a natural, you'll have to work hard just to learn the basics. Even if you're younger, more flexible, and more athletic than I am, you may not progress as quickly as you might wish. And whereas I had the luxury of unlimited access to Sandra Post's expertise, guidance, and encouragement (although, as she points out in her prologue, I rarely had her undivided attention), you will have to settle for a few lessons from a pro, followed by a gradual learning-curve through practice, practice, practice, reinforced by dipping into books of instruction such as this one, watching and rewatching instructional videos, and picking up pointers from a golf partner further along the road than you. One hundred months is probably a more realistic timeline than one hundred days to become really acquainted with this exhilarating and maddening game.

However long your golf journey takes is immaterial in the end. Because the nature of the journey – the triumphs, the failures, the progress, and the setbacks – is endlessly the same. Learning to play golf is not like learning to ride a bicycle. It's not like learning to read. It's not like learning to drive a car. It's not, in other words, something you learn step by step until you've got it – once and for all. Over the five-hundred-year history of this storied game, not a single golfer has progressed in a straight line from triumph to triumph. Setbacks, frustrations, humiliations are an integral part of the game.

Brilliant golfer that she is, Sandra Post knows this. She asked me to write about my introduction to golf because she was sure that the hundreds of golfers, both new and experienced, that she teaches in her School of Golf would identify with a story like mine. It's easy to find golf-instruction texts in a bookstore, Sandra observed, but she'd never been able to find a true story about a real golfer taking up the game for the first time. She told me to write a *story*, not a manual, a story other students of golf could read – and sympathize with or groan over – in bed or in a favourite chair.

Improvements, when they happen, happen bit by bit. Four weeks after my first lesson, I felt invincible for one brief, transcendental day. "At last," I trumpeted, "I've taken a giant leap forward." My husband, David, who took his first golf lesson at age sixteen, congratulated me and then added quickly, "The trick is to build on this moment. Golf is such a game of nanomillimetres. You improve by tiny increments. And you must play regularly to add to these increments." Alas, life intervenes, and the increments melt away. And from time to time they suffer sudden, disastrous meltdowns. Every golfer goes through the same cycle, which is one reason Sandra left me alone much more often than I would have liked, to experience on my own the highs and the lows she knows lie endlessly in wait.

Golf is a journey with no end in sight for any player, even for the Tiger Woodses and the Sandra Posts of this world. It will gladden your heart, and madden, frustrate, and defeat you. Until tomorrow. Scarlett O'Hara should have been a golfer because, in golf, tomorrow is always another day.

ANTICIPATION

CHAPTER 1

TRUE CONFESSIONS OF
A RELUCTANT GOLFER

To say I was a golf beginner is something of an understatement. Let me explain. Although I've spent twenty-five of the past thirty years married to avid golfers (with a five-year hiatus between two marriages), I assiduously avoided picking up a club or learning even the basic rudiments of the game.

Playing golf as far as I was concerned was shorthand for Gone Fishing (read: Goofing Off). At the apex of my hierarchy of golf stereotypes was the retiree in a loud shirt and yellow pants, who does "nothing much now except play golf" – in other words, zip. Close behind came the younger, overpaid, out-of-shape businessman, given to doing deals on a motorized golf cart. Then there were retired American presidents (from Eisenhower to Ford to Bush) and aging Hollywood actors (from Hope and Crosby to Connery and Eastwood), who grinned affably on the golf course in press photos. *Hello, world! Can't you see I'm having the time of my life?*

When it came to the amount of time my husbands spent on the golf course, my disposition rapidly soured. A golf game took the better part of an entire day, for heaven's sake, while *I* spent every day rushing from one task to the next. The prospect of four or six uninterrupted hours pursuing a little white ball, far from the demands of family, office, house, telephone – followed by several more leisurely hours over drinks with friends – was as remote a possibility for me as a three-month, round-the-world cruise.

So how did the world take such a dramatic turn, you ask? Well, as the Mafia says, things change. My kids grew up, I turned fifty, my job description softened. I still had more than enough to do to fill my days, but time was no longer the enemy. The turning point came during a March Break golf holiday with friends. I had gone along as a non-golfer, content to spend my time walking the beach, reading, and picking up the odd tennis game. On the last day, Dianne, the other wife in our foursome, invited me to accompany her around the golf course while she played. I was reluctant to accept her invitation, but said yes in the spirit of the holiday.

The golf course – a peaceful, pine-clad public course in North Carolina – was virtually empty. As Dianne and I walked from hole to hole, she quietly talked. "You really should give it a try, Loral," she said. "David's going to retire soon, and you're not getting any younger. If you don't take up golf, you'll find yourself spending more and more time alone. *I* ignored golf for years for all the same reasons you have, but Andy loves the game so much I decided to take it up. What I've discovered is that it's a game I can enjoy with Andy and friends or with *my* friends or on my own. I enjoy it all, but, when it really comes down to it, I prefer golfing with women friends. Women are more relaxed, less competitive – they just *enjoy* the game more. Look at those two," she said, pointing to David and Andy, who were standing disconsolately on the next green. Neither was looking at the other, and they were both frowning. "You see, they take it far too seriously! As far as *we're* concerned," Dianne continued, "we can look around and enjoy the day and where we are. Sure, I work at my game and I can get *very* angry with myself at times. I give up golf regularly! It's a bit like giving up smoking – you keep going back to it. In the end I just enjoy it as much as I can and take one game at a time."

It was a cool spring day and the silence and peace and beauty of the course filled me. For the first time ever, I allowed myself to imagine spending several hours in a place like this, following a little white ball from hole to hole. I decided to give golf a chance.

"So you think you might take up golf?" David said, a trace of scepticism in his voice. "Well, that's fine – but you *must* take lessons. You can hack away at tennis and have some fun, but you can't at golf. It'd be a waste of time. You'll develop bad habits, and you won't take the game seriously. First you'll giggle and then you'll give it up before you've finished your second round."

From time to time, David had taken refresher lessons from Sandra Post. Whenever he did, he returned home glowing with praise for Sandra's teaching skills and bursting with renewed determination to improve his game.

"I'll line you up with Sandra," David decreed. "Leave it to me."

And so this book was born.

Here's what I knew and didn't know when I decided to give golf a try. I knew that golf courses, for whatever reason, consisted of nine or eighteen "holes"; that the object of the game was to get a tiny white ball into each of those little holes, one after the other; and that there was a "par" for each hole, which meant a prescribed, optimum number of strokes to get the ball into the hole. I knew that golf's supreme triumph was scoring a "hole in one." It was obvious why a hole in one was regarded with such reverence: landing such a tiny ball in a correspondingly tiny hole, from what seemed an intercontinental distance away, seemed frankly impossible.

I also knew, more or less, what the following terms meant: golf course, golf game, golf ball, golf club, golf bag, golf cart, golf swing. And putter. So I knew what "putt" and "putting" meant. "Tee" and "teeing off" were a bit murky. A golf tee was that little wooden extended-thumbtack-thingamajig that I was forever finding – sometimes in pairs, sometimes in threes – on the kitchen counter, on the stairs, lurking in bathroom cupboards, hidden in drawers under the underwear. But a "tee" was a place on a golf course, too, was it not? And then there were terms such as "tee time" and "teeing off" that were frequently thrown around. The "green" sounded straightforward enough – until I realized it had nothing to do with "fairway," which was also green but had a different function entirely. I was reluctant to ask anyone about precise definitions. I figured they would consider explaining these terms to be something like trying to explain what a golf ball was.*

Remarkably, given the above, the terms "rough" and "sand bunker" were not mysterious to me. The rough was the part of the golf course that wasn't mowed. Wasn't that obvious? And sand bunkers were just what the words implied – depressions filled with sand – and were dotted around golf courses in unpredictable spots. The term didn't baffle me, but the reason for sand bunkers did. In my twenty-five years of second-hand golf, I'd overheard a great deal of chestbeating about "getting out of sand." Why, for heaven's sake, were these irritating obstacles deliberately built in the middle of golf courses' beautiful green expanses? The rough and the trees were different: they were just there. Obviously they were to be avoided, the way you try not to hit a tennis ball over the fence. But building a sand bunker right in the middle of that lovely mown grass seemed as stupid as deliberately digging a pothole in the middle of a tennis court and then instructing tennis players to try to avoid it.

Apart from par (below par, up to par) and hole in one, scoring terms refused to stick in my mind. The two I overheard most often were "bogey" and "birdie," both of which struck me as supremely silly names. I could never remember which was more coveted, a bogey or a birdie. And wasn't there another word, equally off-the-wall, also related to birds? Yes, an eagle. I had no idea what *that* meant. And there was another one, much rarer and even more bizarre: an albatross. Talk about absurd.

---

* *See* Glossary for definitions of golf terms.

I understood the basic concept of trying to get the ball in the hole in as few "strokes" as possible, and that it followed therefore that the lower your score, the better your game. But I didn't know what a golf handicap meant – although I'd certainly heard the term bandied about enough. Other terms I didn't have the faintest understanding of were: drivers, woods, irons, and wedges. A club was a club was a club, was it not?

I hardly need add that terms such as chipping, pitching, hooking, slicing, fading, and on and on and on were *terra incognita*. I didn't know the difference between match play and stroke play; I didn't know what a scramble was. And I certainly didn't know anything about the arcane mysteries of a proper golf grip, or the names of the different parts of a golf club, or the ramifications of correct body position when preparing to "address" the ball, or the components of a golf swing.

Golf gloves were a mystery to me. For years, I'd absent-mindedly picked up dirty, crumpled-up golf gloves in odd places, under the front seat of the car, say, or smothered in dustballs under the bed. They were usually made of thin leather, punctured with holes across the knuckles, which rendered them useless for serious protection or warmth. Obviously they had no purpose beyond sartorial posturing, I decided. So whenever I found one, my instinct was to throw it out immediately – especially since there was always one missing.

And then there were golf clothes. In the course of a normal day at work or play, both my husbands dressed reasonably well, albeit conservatively. They would never choose garish colours such as red or green pants, let alone loud plaids or matching checks. But on the golf course? Such outfits, it seemed, were part of the drill. What was it about this odd game that seemed to destroy people's taste the moment they stepped onto a course?

And the final absurdity: the pom-poms that people pulled over the tops (bottoms?) of their golf clubs. Whatever were they for . . . to keep them *warm*? Some of them were unbearably cute and reminded me of the frilly toilet-roll covers you see at home craft shows. Pom-poms were, I knew, the loving gifts of devoted golf wives who spent long winter nights contentedly crocheting and knitting and embroidering these warm fuzzies for their hubbies. It was all too much.

My devotion extended as far as hoisting my husband's golf bag up from the floor, where he had unceremoniously dropped it the minute he came through the front door, then lugging it through our narrow city house and stuffing it into a closet out of the way of traffic. I didn't always succeed; we very nearly ended up in divorce court one recent fall when David announced that, *this* winter, he wanted his clubs prominently displayed in our kitchen "to remind me of summer."

Through the many years that I tuned golf out, I subliminally absorbed a few clues about this "game of games" (David's phrase). For one: I was aware that golfers could animatedly "talk golf" for what seemed hours at a time. In a way that you could never talk tennis, for example. The minute detail with which they remembered particular swings and scores at particular holes amazed me.

I had noticed that people I hugely admired for other reasons were, inexplicably, dedicated golfers. People such as Canada's veteran broadcaster and author Peter Gzowski, who is one of my cultural icons. And I couldn't keep shoving under the rug the fact that I had married not one but two enthusiastic golfers. Apart from their annoying devotion to the game – when they knew there was work to be done! – I couldn't criticize either of them for a lack of energy or imagination in their day-to-day lives.

As I dipped my toe into the foreign world of golf, I noticed to my mild surprise that I warmed to the people I was meeting. When I called the Golf Gap, a golf paraphernalia shop in Toronto, the person who answered the phone was genuinely interested in my request, as well as informed, helpful, and engaging. Hardly the run-of-the-mill clerk who routinely picks up a store phone. And I began to remember past brushes with golf and golfers, such as the conscientious and compassionate Scottish doctor I interviewed a few years back, who confided that the only thing that kept him sane from week to week as he negotiated his stressful private practice were his Thursday afternoons on the Turnberry golf course, site of countless British Opens. His regular time on the course was so essential to his mental balance, he said, that he made it an inviolable rule to be there, "barring death, the plague, or vomiting of blood in gallons."

And I remembered David's and my fleeting visit one fall to golf's Holy Grail, St. Andrew's Royal and Ancient golf course in Scotland. We stopped by the lobby of the old, gracious Rusack's Hotel, which faces the 17th fairway. On impulse, David asked a desk clerk if there were any rooms available during the British Open the following summer. "I'm sorry, sir," the clerk replied gravely, without a trace of dismissiveness or impatience in his voice. "I'm afraid we don't have any rooms available at that time."

David digested this reply for a moment and then said, more to himself than anyone, "Yes, yes, of course. I imagine you fill up early for the Open."

"I'm afraid so, sir," the clerk replied, again without irony or superciliousness. "We've been booked for three years." The rooms during the Open cost exactly the same as they did normally. Although the opportunity to do so was obvious, this venerable hotel situated on the world's most historic golf course saw no need to profiteer just because they could. Golf, it seemed, harked back to an honourable tradition of civility, unpretentiousness, and humility. I didn't know it at the time, but I'd just had my first golf lesson.

CHAPTER 2

TIGERMANIA IGNITES
THE MASTERS

David watches golf on television fairly often, but it's not an obsession the way TV football or hockey is with some men. With one exception: the Masters. For David, the Masters is the Holy Grail, True Religion, the Way, the Truth, and the Life. During the four days in April that the Masters golf tournament is played every year in Augusta, Georgia, David's other life stops. *Nothing* takes precedence. He accepts no invitations, anywhere. The TV set is his closest friend.

This year, encouraged by my resolution to take up golf, David decreed a Masters party for his golfing cronies. Well, I might as well get into the spirit of it all, I thought nervously. Were golf-watching parties like Super Bowl parties, I wondered. How was *I* to know? I resolved to just go with the flow.

The four-day event started slowly, as did Tiger Woods' game. On Thursday, I joined David in front of the TV at 5 P.M. We were alone: the Masters TV-In with

David's buddies would begin on Saturday. I tried my best to pay attention and concentrate on what was happening, but when the network signed off after a little more than an hour, I was relieved to regain my freedom.

On Friday, I watched for two hours. I found I could concentrate fairly well if I focused on Tiger's game. The obvious star quality of this handsome young American of African and Thai heritage was starting to work on me. He looked fabulous in his Nike duds – a matching royal-blue cap and shirt that looked terrific against his burnished skin. I knew he was in the lead, but I didn't appreciate yet how spectacular his lead was shaping up to be.

On Saturday, the party began. I arrived home from some errands half an hour after TV coverage started to find Andy and Dianne settled in with David in front of the TV, a bottle of Scotch on the coffee table. I was grateful to see Dianne. "I'm trying hard to get into this," I confided, "but my mind wanders a lot."

"Well, of course it does!" Dianne replied with comforting matter-of-factness. She was not surprised? "No, it's *hard* to keep track. You have to really concentrate. And you have to pay attention all the time. It took me *years* to get to the point where I could watch golf for any extended period of time without my mind wandering."

Reassured, I relayed some of the amazing discoveries I'd made watching with David on Thursday and Friday. Things such as finding out that the flagstick on the green was routinely moved from day to day. I was stunned to learn that new holes were made *all the time* – and not just for big tournaments like this, but on every golf course! I had simply assumed that all eighteen holes were carved in stone, so to speak.

The Tiger Triumph was building. We were all mesmerized by him. His focus, concentration, and ability to screen out distractions were awesome to watch. In an interview after his first round, which was just short of impressive, Tiger talked about "digging down deep" and "knowing exactly what I have to do tonight" – a series of "reps" (repeated strokes) in order to imprint them on his mind and his swing the following day. He stated this goal with a businesslike directness and consummate confidence that would make anyone – even me, the quintessential golf ignoramus – sit up and listen. I had never witnessed such deep inner certainty, obviously genuine and *on TV*. As a desultory student of yoga myself, I was slack-jawed. Was this a *golfer* before me, who not only played the game according to the purest principles of yoga but was able to clearly articulate them as well?

By the end of Saturday's round, Tiger was an invincible nine shots in the lead. Tomorrow would be Tiger's day, David and Andy predicted, looking more than a little stunned. We were all in Tiger's thrall.

On Sunday, I welcomed the golf gang, about eight people today. Our crowded living room crackled with Tiger-talk and Tiger-awe. Ken Rodmell, a long-time golf partner of David's whom David reveres as a thoughtful, immensely knowledgeable golfer, asked the assembled group if they'd ever played their best game over eighteen holes – one brief, shining game during which their swing, their putting, and their mental focus all came together to form a perfect game. Everyone shook their heads glumly. Then Ken turned to David and asked him very, very casually how he will feel if his wife beats him at golf after her upcoming Sandra Post lessons. David turned up the volume on the TV.

The next morning, Monday, April 14, 1997, Tigermania grips the world. Not only has Tiger won the Masters, he's broken every record in the book. Just twenty-one, he's the youngest player ever to win the Masters; he's shot the lowest score in the tournament's sixty-one-year history; he's won by twelve strokes, the widest margin ever of any major golf tournament; and he is the first black man to win a major professional golf title. "No longer can anyone say that golf is for old fogeys," David crows over the morning newspapers. Sure enough, the tiny, lurking feeling that taking up golf meant I was saying goodbye to my youth with finality has disappeared. Tiger has banished it forever.

I'm psyched for my golf lessons with Sandra Post. They start in two weeks. What a marvellous omen Tiger is for my fledgling game! All of a sudden golf has panache, zip. Drama and suspense, too. "I suppose Tiger will just win and win and win now," I murmur, as I scan a *New York Times* story that heralds "WOODS A MASTER IN THE OLD SOUTH."

"Of course he will *not*!" David harrumphs. "Golf is a game of nanomillimetres. The tiniest thing can interfere with your game. Sure, he'll win more tournaments, probably many more, over the next twenty, or thirty, years. But he won't win tournament after tournament after tournament, non-stop – not even right now." He delivers this dictum with cantankerous certainty.

"Hmmph," I retort, and think to myself, What does he really know?

I remember Ken Rodmell's unanswered question and smile inwardly.

CHAPTER 3

RAW BEGINNINGS

In games . . . problems are solved, somebody wins. Hence the 'isle of joy'
offered by sport in an ocean of anxieties. I have come to feel a deep, unspoken
pity for people who have no attachment to a single sport, almost as sorry for
them as I am for teetotallers.

– British-American journalist Alistair Cooke, eighty-nine,
who was persuaded by his wife to take up golf in his fifties
so that he wouldn't end up a "typewriter arthritic."

My cousin Sharon, exactly the same age as I am and my friend since we were toddlers, has signed up with me for my first Sandra Post golf clinic. I had suggested we take lessons together; it seemed like an excellent idea a few weeks ago. But now that Day One, April 29, is upon me, I'm wondering why I've complicated things for myself. Sharon has been playing golf off and on for years with her husband,

Rick. Sharon *says* she doesn't know much, really needs lessons, etc., etc. But frankly, I doubt it. Sharon is very quiet and very private; and she does everything very slowly, very precisely, and very well. This includes any sport she tackles. She doesn't look like an athlete: she's small-boned, with a willowy frame that looks fragile. This is an optical illusion! She's strong and sinewy, and whenever we play tennis, Sharon quietly, efficiently beats me. Damn! I wish I were going alone. I really do *not* want witnesses to this golf thing. I do *not* want to be consistently, quietly, efficiently shown up. I remember telling Sharon on the phone last night how excited I am that we're doing this together. What a fraud I am.

I'm supposed to pick her up at 9 A.M. She's not ready when I get there, and I use the five minutes I wait, motor idling, to work myself into a froth of righteous indignation. I really do *not* want to be late on my first day, and I don't know if it will take forty-five minutes or an hour and forty-five minutes to get to "the Golf Ranch," home of the Sandra Post School of Golf. The Golf Ranch is away the hell west out Highway 401 and then north some – what else to expect from a golf school? Traffic is a nightmare on the 401 almost any time day or night these days. Hurry up, Sharon.

Sharon emerges, cool, together, unapologetic, lugging a giant golf bag. Immediately, I feel diminished. I, of course, do not have a single club. I was assured when I signed up for the clinic that there would be plenty of "demo" clubs, but now I wonder if I got that piece of information right. "I just bought these clubs with our insurance money," Sharon announces as she slides into the passenger seat. "Both Richard's and mine were stolen out of our trunk. Four thousand dollars worth of clubs down the tube."

"*Four thousand dollars?*" I gasp.

"Yes, Loral," Sharon replies, cocking one of her perfect eyebrows. "You can spend much more than *that* on clubs if you want to. Big Berthas sell for six hundred dollars *each*." *Big Berthas?* I exhale noisily and lurch into second gear, reminded of why I've avoided this ridiculous rich-man's sport for so many years.

Sharon guides me expertly to the 401 via a route I didn't know existed, and we arrive fifteen minutes before the clinic begins. The Golf Ranch proves much less grand than I had imagined from its name. It looks like a glorified driving range, hold the glory. There's a long stretch of practice tees lined up across an empty field, a small wooden building with a rudimentary snack bar/reception area inside, and, next door, a tiny wooden shed emblazoned with the Sandra Post School of Golf on one side. The entire operation is smack up against Highway 10, a four-lane ribbon of highway stretching northward into the heartland of rural Ontario. Somehow I'd thought that *Sandra Post* – Sports Hall of Famer, Athlete of the Year, etc., etc., one of those legendary Canada's Darlings right up there with Barbara Ann Scott, Marilyn Bell, Nancy Greene – would operate out of something . . . well, not *this*.

Sharon takes her golf bag out of the trunk and we approach the sign. It's a sunny, cool day, maybe 15°C – reasonable weather for the end of April, I'd thought when I left the house. But the *wind* out here on this blasted heath is something else. I look around and realize there's nothing to break it: no trees, just a flat expanse of farmers' fields all round and that north-south highway slashing through the barrens and thundering with twenty-two-wheelers.

"Hello!" The stocky, forty-something woman behind the voice and the mass of dead-straight streaked blonde hair spilling over a white visor looks instantly familiar. Canada's Darling is a vision of sporty flair. She's wearing a fuzzy forest-green sweatshirt, matching pants, white turtleneck, and green-and-white saddle-style golf shoes that tie the ensemble together. I look down uneasily at my borrowed windbreaker, khaki pants, and scuffed tennis shoes. Sandra sizes me up with a quick glance and says, "You need a club." I give her a quick once-over back as I accept the club she hands me. Hmmm. I peg her as a study in restless energy and bonhomie. My stepdaughter would take a long, hard look at her and pronounce her "the goods." The goods introduces Sharon and me to our fellow students: Terry, a round-faced, solidly built woman with short grey hair – in her early fifties, I'd say; and Janet, steaming towards us from the parking lot, lugging a giant golf bag and looking at her watch. Janet, about forty-five, has streaky red hair pulled back into a makeshift ponytail, and she knows she's late. I'm vaguely comforted: Janet looks as frazzled as I feel.

"That's it, then," Sandra says briskly. "We're a small class today. Let's get started, shall we? It's been a long winter, and we all need to stretch out."

We stand around in a half-circle while Sandra demonstrates a few stretching exercises. To my surprise, I find these exercises quite challenging. I've clung to the notion that the one thing golf does not require is physical fitness. Could I be wrong?

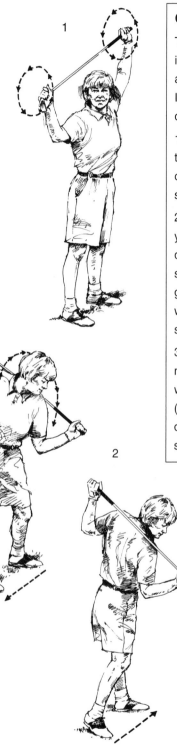

GOLF WARM-UP EXERCISES

The golf swing requires flexibility and, the older we get, the more inflexible we become. Players frequently arrive for their golf game after work or a long drive with tight shoulders and a stiff lower back. It's important to warm up these muscles and stretch them out. If you don't, you can hurt yourself.

1. Hold one of your woods or long irons above your head, parallel to the ground, arms slightly behind your shoulders. Then twirl each end of the golf club in small backward circles. This helps stretch out your shoulders and pectorals.

2. Put your golf club across your *shoulders* (not your neck) and rotate your shoulders on a slant around your spine, turning first one shoulder towards an imaginary ball and then the other, maintaining the slant. Do not turn back and forth with your shoulders parallel to the ground. This is a turn used in tennis or baseball. Be aware of the weight shift. Load to the right; unload to the left. Keep head still. Feel shoulders rotating around spine.

3. Swing two golf clubs together in a loose backward and forward motion. Start with a small swing, gradually increasing it. The extra weight (in addition to the swing) helps stretch out your back muscles. (For the added weight, you can also use a leaded "donut," which slips down the shaft of the golf club. Donuts are sold at most discount and sports stores.)

Twirling the golf club in tiny *backward* circles while holding it above your shoulders looks dead easy. It's not. The tightness and tension I feel up my neck and across my shoulders and upper back are excruciating. And bending each shoulder down towards an imaginary ball with a golf club across my upper back gives my spine and upper back a twist they're not accustomed to. And I thought yoga had made me flexible! When Sandra counsels me to shift my weight to the right foot while I lean to the left, and vice versa, I'm flummoxed. When I lean to the left, I want to shift my weight to the left. Not right. "No, Loral," Sandra says drily as she corrects me, "it's your *other* left shoulder that points down." Ouch.

While we nurse our stretched-out muscles, Sandra launches into a show and tell about the contents of her golf bag, a gleaming red-and-white affair with SANDRA POST down one side. She stands facing us beside her impressive bag, pulling out club after club and putting each one back, all the time talking at dizzying speed about what each one is called, what it's used for, and things about "loft," "shaft length," "trajectory," and distance.

I am completely lost. I steal a furtive glance around the group and see that everyone else is listening tight and nodding wisely. Well, I console myself nervously, they all have golf clubs of their own, so of course they understand all of this better than I do.

Knowing my lessons were about to begin, I've really, truly tried to get a leg up on golf terminology over the past couple of months by reading how-to golf manuals. One of the standard things these books drill into you is the difference between irons and woods: *woods are for distance, irons are for accuracy.* So far, so good. But then I wade into murky waters, namely: the basic rule about golf-club numbers, which is "The higher the number, the shorter the club." It would be so much easier if it were the other way round, would it not? Why shouldn't a 9-iron be the longest club and a 1-iron the shortest? (A dismissive "because it just isn't, that's all" is all David can offer.) Especially since the higher the number, the greater the "loft," or angle, of the clubface. Which means that shorter clubs, with higher numbers, have greater lofts, and therefore send the ball higher – but not as *far* as the longer clubs, with lower numbers and lower lofts . . . which send the ball lower and farther. *Right?*

As if all this isn't confusing enough, the differences between irons and woods have to be sorted out, of course. I *have* figured out that woods are the bigger, fatter fellows (although they are no longer made of wood, Sandra explains . . . well, this

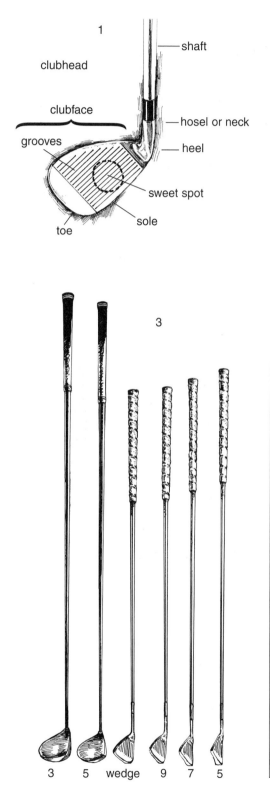

1

shaft

clubhead

clubface

grooves

hosel or neck

heel

sweet spot

sole

toe

3

3   5   wedge   9   7   5

GOLF CLUBS

1. PARTS OF A GOLF CLUB

Before you learn your way around a golf course, you need to know your way around your golf clubs! Here are the names of each part of your golf club: clubhead, clubface, sweet spot, grooves, sole, toe, heel, hosel or neck, shaft.

2. ASSORTMENT OF GOLF CLUBS

You are allowed to carry fourteen clubs – maximum – in your golf bag. There is no minimum. A full set of clubs can be assembled from any combination of:

driver or 1-wood	1- or 2-iron (rarely used by women)
3-wood	3-iron
4-wood	4-iron
5-wood	5-iron
7-wood	6-iron
	7-iron
9-wood	8-iron
	9-iron
11-wood	pitching wedge
	sand wedge
	L or lob wedge (for very good players)
	putter

But when you are starting the game, seven clubs are enough. Having fewer clubs to choose from will make learning easier.

3. A HALF-SET OF CLUBS FOR THE NEW GOLFER

3-wood (to use for your tee shot)
5-wood (to use off the fairway)
pitching wedge or sand wedge (your choice)
8-iron or 9-iron (short iron)
6-iron or 7-iron (middle iron)
4-iron or 5-iron (long iron)
putter (opposite page)

The longest club in your bag (your 3- or 5-wood) should hit the ball the farthest. You use this club from the tee and on long fairway shots. As you near the green, you use irons. The higher the number on the club, the more loft; this should put higher trajectory on the ball, but the ball will not travel as far.

SANDRA TALKS ABOUT LEFT-HANDED GOLFERS

Canada has more left-handed golfers per capita than any other country in the world. Instruction described in our book is for right handers. Left handers must reverse the instruction to match their swing.

hardly surprises me. I'm past expecting anything about this game to be logical). But you use woods to "tee off" with, because you want to hit the ball as far as you can, right? But that tee-off shot, the shot that epitomizes golf and golfing, has a nice soaring "loft" to it, does it not?

So what's my problem? Well, Sandra said today (one thing I did retain) that *woods are longer than irons.* Which presumably means *all* woods are longer than *all* irons – even the longest iron, which is to say, the one with the smallest number, the 1-iron (well, 2-iron – apparently hardly anyone carries a 1-iron). So long woods produce high lofts, right? But this contradicts the irons rule stated above, that *the shorter the club, the higher the loft.*

Just writing this down gives me a tension headache.

"Lighten up!" David says this evening when I lay all this on him over a drink. "Have a little patience. It will all come miraculously clear when you actually get out there and start to hit some balls. You'll see."

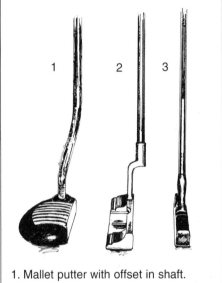

1. Mallet putter with offset in shaft.

2. Flange putter with offset shaft (this helps you keep your hands ahead of the ball).

3. Blade putter with straight shaft.

Our beginners' clinic continues with the parts of a golf club. I recover my equilibrium during this short session, thanks to my studious reading of golf manuals. For a moment I'm actually the star pupil, barking out answers as Sandra points to various parts of the club – heel, toe, clubface, sweet spot, neck or hosel, shaft, grip.

We're ready now for the meat of the lesson: the Four Basics of Golf: Grip, Stance, Posture, and Alignment. Sandra introduces the Four Basics with a short talk about why they're essential to a good golf swing. She cannot overemphasize their importance, she says. I'm not surprised. From my reading, I've gathered that Grip, Stance, Posture, and Alignment – all of which happen before you even hit the ball – are the Catechism of Golf. Every book I've picked up pounds these basics home, stressing that they're essential to a successful golf swing. In my heart of hearts, I wonder about this. Could this, perhaps, be some sort of elaborate initiation rite into the Inner Sanctum of Golf? Why don't you just stand up there and hit the damn ball? Could a maverick – or someone like Sandra with natural talent in every single moving part of her body – simply ignore these basics and get away with it?

Sandra leaves no room for such heretical thoughts. She makes it clear that she truly believes in *her* heart of hearts that the Four Basics are the basis of a good swing. And to drive home her point, she adds that they are even more important for women than they are for men, because we lack simple, unadulterated muscle power: "Women can't get away with a bad swing the way some men can, through sheer muscle power."

My inner doubts notwithstanding, I knuckle down. I know that, even though Tiger was a child prodigy and a natural talent, he has practised and practised, and trained and trained. And I'm far too insecure – not to mention being a bookish sort who's used to following the rules – to strike out on my own, swinging wildly, confident that I'll do okay.

And so to work.

THE GRIP

Sandra demonstrates three standard grips: the Baseball (or Ten-Finger) Grip, which is simple and straightforward but not often recommended; the Interlocking Grip, the grip Jack Nicklaus and Tiger Woods use (this one feels the most secure for beginners, says Sandra); and the Overlapping (or Vardon) Grip, the grip of choice for 97 per cent of the Tour players, Sandra says.

I try out the Interlocking and the Overlapping grips (Sandra makes it clear we're not to choose the Baseball Grip unless we have some special problem, such as arthritis) and settle on the Interlocking Grip. It feels weird and unnatural, but it does feel secure, just as she predicted. And besides, what's good enough for Jack Nicklaus and Tiger Woods is good enough for me.

THE FOUR BASICS OF GOLF

1.THE GRIP

A good grip means that the hands work together as a unit. Whichever grip you choose, hold on to the club firmly but not tightly. Beginners often develop a white-knuckle grip, with tension running up their forearms and into their shoulders. Relax!

There are three different types of grips to choose from. The most popular grip among professional golfers is the Overlapping (or Vardon) Grip. New golfers often choose the Interlocking Grip, because it feels secure, although they often grip the club too tightly when they use this one. Tour pros Nancy Lopez and Tiger Woods use the Interlocking Grip. The disadvantage of the Baseball (or Ten-Finger) Grip is that the hands may not work together as a unit. Its advantage is that it may help you release your hands during the swing. We recommend the Baseball Grip for junior golfers with small hands or golfers with arthritis in their hands, elbows, or shoulders. Canadian golf pros Moe Norman and Dave Barr use the Baseball Grip.

Experiment with all three grips until you feel comfortable with one of them. To find a good grip:

1. Stand upright with your hands hanging naturally by your sides.

2. Grasp the club in your left hand, diagonally from the heel of your palm to the base of your forefinger.

3. Wrap your fingers around the club with your thumb slightly to the right of centre on the shaft. You should be able to see two knuckles of your left hand. The thumb and forefinger of your left hand should form a V that points towards your right shoulder.

4. Place your right hand directly below your left hand with your left thumb covered by the pad at the base of the thumb of your right hand.

1

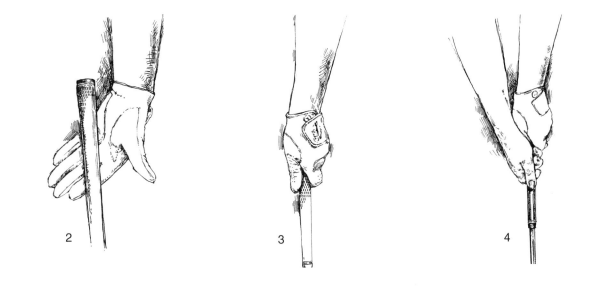

2   3   4

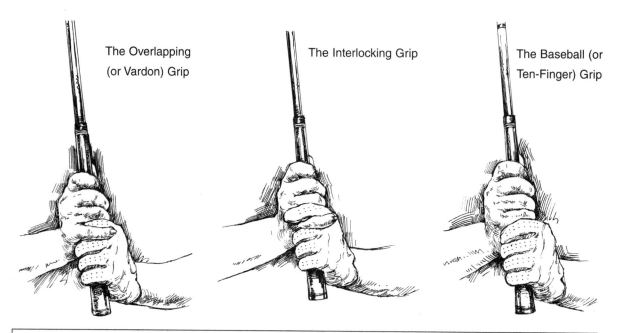

The Overlapping
(or Vardon) Grip

The Interlocking Grip

The Baseball (or
Ten-Finger) Grip

The Overlapping (or Vardon) Grip

The baby finger of your right hand fits comfortably on top of your left hand, between your forefinger and your middle finger.

The Interlocking Grip

Your right baby finger interlocks with the forefinger of your left hand.

The Baseball (or Ten-Finger) Grip

As the name implies, all ten fingers are on the club. Your hands should touch each other (the thumb of your left hand is covered by the pad at the base of your right thumb).

Sandra's Tip: Your "grip" also refers to the rubber sheath around your clubshaft. It's very important that this grip is the right size for you. Your fingers should barely touch the other side of your hand when you grasp it.

Maintaining Your Grip: The grip on your club should be changed every twenty-five rounds or once a season, because of weather, oils from your hands, and normal wear. To help your grips wear longer, you can wash them with water and a brush every few rounds.

Sandra has given each of us our own "golf station," with a metal rack to stand our clubs against, facing the driving range. We're lined up now, holding our clubs in whichever grip feels best. "Now no matter what I tell you, you're going to hold on to that club for dear life!" Sandra adds. "Which is fine to start, but I want you to remember one thing every time you grip your club: Hold on to it the way you would hold on to a baby bird. You want to be sure you don't let go and that you're in control, but you don't want to smother that baby bird."

She demonstrates her grip, the overlapping one, and then asks one of us to take the club out of her hands. I do, and am astonished to find how easily it slips from her grasp. "See what I mean?" she grins. "Relax! Try not to use the death grip!"

STANCE

The stance is a piece of cake. You just stand in a balanced position, with your feet the same width apart as your shoulders and your weight evenly distributed between both feet. *This* feels perfectly natural, unlike the grip.

POSTURE

The posture is trickier than the stance. "Our centre of gravity is in our butt," Sandra opines about women. Too true. But the correct golf posture in which we must "address" the ball (such Victorian-sounding terminology!) involves bending from the *hips* rather than the waist, then sticking your butt out. This is not easy: bending from my waist feels much more natural. And there are two other things to factor into this unnatural-feeling, but apparently "correct," posture: We're to keep our backs straight – hips to shoulders – and unlock our knees.

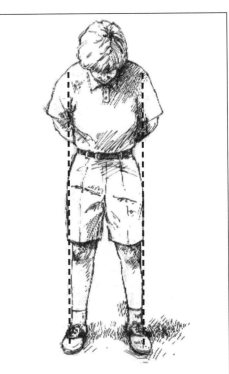

2. STANCE

The stance is the foundation of the golf swing. Simply take an athletic stance, with your feet about shoulder-width (slightly wider when you use woods). Keep your weight evenly distributed between your two feet and your toes slightly flared to help you transfer weight. Your knees should flex comfortably, towards your toes. If your feet are too close together, you won't have good balance, and if they're too wide apart, it will restrict your turn.

Correct

3. POSTURE

Stand tall and bend to the ball from your hips. Unlock your knees to counterbalance the bend. Notice how straight your spine is from your hips to your neck. Your arms will fall naturally from your shoulders when you grasp your club.

Do *not* bend from your waist as if you are sitting; or feel pressure on your thighs, as if you were skiing. This may hurt your back and does not allow proper shoulder/hip turn to occur.

Sandra's Tip: Of the Four Basics, the posture is misunderstood most often. But if you concentrate on standing tall and then bending from the hip sockets, you'll be fine. *Do not sit!* If you do, you'll limit your shoulder turn when you swing and have a difficult time getting the ball in the air. Your centre of gravity should be in your butt.

Incorrect

1-3

Set-up, or Address, Position

1. The left shoulder is higher than the right. This helps keep the left arm straight, not locked or hyper-extended. Your two arms form a V.

2. The shaft should be on a slight angle; the clubface is square to the target.

3. The hands are even with the ball.

4. The distance of the club from the body is approximately one hand-width for a mid-length iron (7- or 6-iron). As the club gets longer, the distance from the body increases slightly.

Note: The Fourth Basic, Alignment, is on page 48.

4

To demonstrate the straight-back part of the posture, Sandra stands sideways to us, holding a golf club straight down her back. Easier said than done. I wiggle around, pushing out my butt, unlocking my knees . . . or, rather, trying to. Sandra inspects us and tells me I'm sitting down instead of bending from my hips. "This is *not* skiing! This is golf," she instructs.

Sharon, drat her, has this down cold. I watch her assume her posture: it is a portrait of slow, measured elegance. First, to see if her back is straight, she carefully places a golf club down her spine. It is. Then she puts down her club and proceeds to "assume her posture." She stands perfectly straight and tall. Then she leans forward – from the hips, of course – spine ramrod straight. She proceeds to unlock her knees and stick her butt out. It all looks graceful, perfectly paced, disciplined.

Meanwhile, my attempt at correct posture feels anything but natural. Nor does it feel comfortable. Already I feel warning twinges in my lower back. I ask Sharon if she feels anything in her back and she says yes, in her *upper* back. No matter what Sandra says about our centre of gravity being in our butt, *I* say sticking your butt out like that looks and feels awkward.

Alignment will come last. We'll leave it until tomorrow, Sandra says. Time to get on with hitting the ball. She starts by showing us how to "tee up" the ball. "I want you to look good," she says. "Especially when you're out there on that first tee and people are watching you. So *this* is how you do it." She picks up a ball and a tee, places them both between her thumb and forefinger, ball on top, and bends down and pushes the tee into the ground using the weight of the ball for leverage. She does it all in one fluid motion. "This is just a little thing," Sandra says, "but it's important. If you try to push the tee into the ground by itself and *then* place the ball on top, likely as not the ball will fall off. And you'll look like a klutz – in front of all those men watching you on the first tee, just waiting for you to look like one!

"We're going to start by gently swinging the club backward and forward just to get the feel of swinging a club," Sandra continues. She swings her club about a foot backward and forward and gently hits the ball she's just teed up. It neatly hits an empty ball bucket she has placed about thirty feet away. "We women are afraid to swing our arms," she says. "For some reason, we think we have to use our bodies. Try to keep your body quiet. Just swing those arms backward and forward."

We all try it. Immediately, I find out why Sandra took such pains to show us how to tee up the ball gracefully. This is not easy, even when I do it the way she has showed us. The silly ball keeps falling off! At last it stays, and I try Sandra's gentle backward-and-forward swing. To my delight, I do fine. Not only do I hit the ball, I actually hit the basket and knock it down! My confidence soars.

TOE IN THE AIR, TOE IN THE AIR

"Now we'll extend this swing to a half-swing," Sandra says. "We call this exercise 'Toe in the Air, Toe in the Air.'"

She assumes her "address" position and places the clubhead flat on the ground in front of her, "in the centre of my stance." Then she swings the club back until it's parallel to the ground. "Look at my clubface," she says. "It's facing straight up, right?" It is. "In other words, the toe is in the air." Right. She swings the club, hits the ball, and brings the club forward to the same position in front of her. "Toe in the air again, right?" Right.

Now she shows us the secret of getting that toe to face straight up. "You must cock your wrists like so. To do it right, the back of your left hand must face forward. Like this.

"So . . . move your arms only, *not* your body. Feel the weight of the club as you bring it down, and go *slowly*: we're *not* looking for speed."

This, alas, is not so easy. I keep turning the clubface forward, instead of holding it perpendicular to the ground. This is happening because I'm not cocking my wrists properly, Sandra tells me. She adjusts my wrists and hands until they're in the correct position. Sure enough, it feels entirely different. But when I try to reproduce this in the middle of my little half-swing, the back of my hand will not obey. It always seems to twist forward. Is this because I have weak wrists? I *am* hitting the ball, however, so not to worry. In fact, it's rolling nicely, straight along the ground in front of me.

But I'm starting to get tired. I decide to take a break and watch my classmates for a few minutes. To my dismay, I see that they're all getting the ball off the ground! And I'd thought I'd been doing just fine, because I was hitting the ball straight. My confidence plummets. I start practising again, and no matter what I do, the silly ball will *not* leave the ground. I seem to be hitting it worse and worse.

And Sandra has decided to concentrate on me for the moment. She stands directly behind me, watching intently. Can't she see I just want to be left alone?

Apparently not. Briskly, she zeroes in on three things: One, I'm not cocking my wrists. Second, I'm moving my body far too much, instead of feeling the weight of the club as it comes down. Third, I'm going too fast. "You're getting panicky," she says. "Just swing the club as slowly as you possibly can. So slowly it feels as if you're never going to get through it."

I take a deep breath and bring the club down slowly, slowly, trying to move it through the arc in one fluid motion. I hit the ball off the ground for the first time. I hear a lovely, unfamiliar sound, a zing, a pin*nng*. It sounds clean. "Yes!" I shout.

My back is aching; my shoulders are stiff. If I hit it again, I fear I may revert to that other, familiar sound: a flat clunk, sort of a dead *thunk*. I decide to call it a day while the lovely pin*nng* is still ringing in my ears.

Sharon is ecstatic on the drive home. She swears she hit more consecutive good balls than she ever has in her life. She attributes this amazing success to breaking down the swing to a half-swing. "In all the golf lessons I've taken over the years, no one has ever taught this before," she says. "I'm going to use this as my fallback swing when I'm having a bad day on the course.

"And, you know what else was different today?" she continues. "This is the first golf lesson I've ever had where things seemed simple. In other lessons, I've always been left feeling there were *so* many things to remember, all at once. This time, it feels so much simpler – and clearer. And Sandra made it fun, don't you think? Of course, all my other teachers have been men. Do you suppose that's the difference?"

Well, I remember Andy and David's glum body language and facial expressions on the golf course in North Carolina. And Dianne's comments about how golfing with women is so much more fun. No, it doesn't surprise me that male teachers may make golf more complicated and much more like work.

I'm absolutely wiped when I get home. I go to bed at 10 P.M. and have a lot of trouble dragging myself out of bed the next day at 7 A.M. When I arrive at Sharon's condo, Rick greets me on the front steps. "Loral! This is a true break-through – *you*, of all people, taking up golf!"

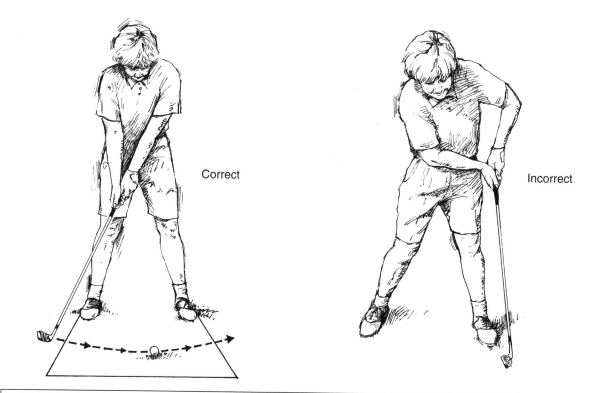

Correct

Incorrect

DEVELOPING THE GOLF SWING

FOUR STEPS TO BUILD A SIMPLE GOLF SWING

Step 1: The Half-Swing

1. Use a 7- or 6-iron.

2. Tee up your ball. It will make learning easier.

3. Take your grip, stance, and posture, including a good set-up that creates a V with your arms.

4. Keep your body still and your wrists solid. Take the club back as far as your right foot, then swing your arms forward to your left foot. *Note:* Be sure to keep your posture and the solid V with your arms and wrists, because if you straighten your posture or pull your arms in, you will top the ball and it will roll along the ground.

Sandra's Tip: Your swing thought should be "Get the ball in the air and hit it straight." To do so, swing slowly. You want the ball to go only ten to fifteen yards. Try to hit the tee or brush the grass. Hit *down* on the ball. Listen for a clicking sound.

Many women have a difficult time letting their arms swing in front of and past their bodies. Maybe it's the way we are built. Women also find it difficult to extend their arms. We constantly pull our arms in towards our body in a diamond shape (as shown above on the right). Perhaps women feel we have to help the ball in the air. We don't. The club is built to do that. Don't be afraid to hit down to get the ball in the air.

wristcock

Step 2: Toe in the Air, Toe in the Air

1. With the same good grip, stance, posture, and set-up, take the club back to just below waist-high.

2. As you take the club back to a parallel position, your left shoulder moves slightly towards the ball.

3. Your left arm is straight, without being locked or hyper-extended, and the back of your left hand is flat and facing in front of you.

4. Your right arm folds and your wrists begin a wristcock.

5. Keeping your body still, start the club back down to your starting position.

6. Your forearms and hands have started to rotate forward. Let them continue to go forward until your right arm is extended and the back of your right hand is facing forward, your left arm is folded, and your right shoulder has moved towards the ball. Your posture is the same, your body remains still, and your eyes are still on the ball.

7. Your grip and forearms may be tightening at this point. Shake out your arms between shots and try to feel the weight of the clubhead.

Sandra's Tip: This waist-high golf swing is a mirror image. What happens on one side happens on the other. You can visualize this as Toe in the Air, Toe in the Air (a mirror image of the clubhead on each side) or Back of the Left Hand Forward, Back of the Right Hand Forward (a wristcock on each side). Take your pick.

SANDRA'S SWING SECRET

HOW I ABSORBED THE GOLF SWING AT GROUND LEVEL

One of the most difficult things to teach in golf is how legs work. I was lucky because I absorbed how to use *my* legs in a very natural way – literally from the ground up. When I was a little girl, I used to hang out with the LPGA players in Florida during our family winter vacations. I was really tiny and I'd sit on the pros' golf bags and watch them on the practice tee from ground level. So I watched their feet and legs a lot. I think that's how I developed my footwork and legwork, and why my feet and legs have always worked so naturally for me.

"Well, as David says, the gods are always laughing," I reply.

"I hear you had a great lesson yesterday," Rick continues. "Sharon was so thrilled about learning that half-swing. . . . You know I've *told* her to do that when she's having problems during a game. But would she listen? You don't suppose it was my tone of voice now, do you?" Rick has a marvellous, self-deprecating sense of humour. And funny he should bring this up: I read an amusing article in one of David's golf magazines last night about how men are compulsive about giving their mates golf tips . . . and about how their advice falls on deaf ears.

We arrive at the Golf Ranch half an hour early. It's another ferociously windy day, and Sandra is standing in her teaching area, buffeted by the wind, giving a private lesson. Terry is taking her golf bag out of her trunk as we arrive, so the three of us agree to share a bucket of balls while we're waiting for our class to begin. I stand behind Terry and watch in awe as she hits ball after ball well past the 150-yard flag. She's a big woman, what the Germans would call *saftig*, solidly built but not fat. And she is strong! Oh well. Back to basics. I hit about ten balls a distance of ten, twenty, and, a couple of times, about fifty yards.

I turn around to check how Sharon is doing, and see that she hasn't started hitting yet. She's methodically going through the stretching exercises we learned yesterday. Oh yes, I should have done those first.

Step 3: The Follow-Through

1. Starting with your good grip, stance, posture, and set-up, take your club back to the Step 2: Toe in the Air position. Be careful not to go past waist-high.

2. Continue on through the forward swing, keeping your eyes on the ground, even after you have hit the ball.

3. Now add the follow-through position, as if it were an afterthought.

4. Keeping your balance when you follow through is important. Since your clubhead speed is very slow, you should find this easy.

What the follow-through looks like: Your weight has moved to your front, or left, foot (the foot closest to the pin). Your back, or right, foot is at a ninety-degree angle to the ground. Your hips and shoulders face the target. Your arms are high, with your hands higher than the clubhead.

Sandra's Tip: If you are finding it difficult to finish in balance, slow your swing down. Finishing in balance is very important to developing a sound golf swing.

Today's class starts with review: grip, stance, posture, half-swing. I'm still having trouble with the wristcock on the half-swing. When Sandra corrects me, it feels totally different – unnatural, my bones feel as if they're going to crack – but it works.

I have a new problem today: what Sandra calls my "incredible footwork. I've *never* seen anything like it! You're bouncing all over the place," she grins. "Shall we nail you to the ground?" I try my damnedest to think, Feet: stay still! But most of the time I'm completely unaware of what my feet are up to. Once, however, I catch myself. It's appalling: I practically follow the ball to the target! Would golf shoes help, I wonder?

After we review the half-swing, Sandra tells us to extend the swing a little, and end by "following through." She demonstrates, and I recognize the classic golf pose that's reproduced in every golf book and magazine: body twisted like a corkscrew, right heel off the ground, club over the shoulder across the back at a nice angle, elbows up, face front, eyes fixed on the middle distance where the ball has

Step 4: The Full Swing

1. Start with your good grip, stance, posture, and set-up. Don't worry about perfecting these four basics. In time, they will come naturally.

2. Take the club back waist-high. The toe of the club is in the air, the back of your left hand faces forward. Continue turning your left shoulder to the ball.

Your body now starts to turn. In a full swing, your shoulders turn *more* than your hips (how much they turn depends on your flexibility).

As your left shoulder turns to the ball, your weight should start to move towards the right side. This can be towards your right thigh or your right foot, whichever is comfortable for you.

3. Your thumbs are going to start to move upwards, facing the sky. It's almost like hitchhiking. Your left arm stays extended (but not locked or hyper-extended), and your right arm folds. *Note:* The right arm can lift upwards; make sure your right elbow faces the ground (this is not a baseball swing).

Take your club back only as far as you feel comfortable. It takes time for your back muscles to stretch out. Many new golfers believe that the farther they take the club back, the farther the ball will go. This is not true. Control of the club is what is important. You do not even have to bring the club back to a parallel position with the ground if this is not comfortable.

If your left heel has lifted (most women *do* lift their left heel), keep the ball of your foot on the ground. At the start of the downswing, drop your left heel to help get the weight moving towards your front foot.

4. Start your hands (or the butt end of the club) down towards the ball. When you start this downswing, try to maintain some angle with your hands. Again, this is the wristcock. It creates leverage on the shaft and harnesses energy, giving power to your swing.

Sandra's Tip: Many new golfers get to the top of their swings and visualize the *clubhead* starting the downswing. If you do that, you will release your wristcock and all your power will be gone. You will be unable to hit *down* on the ball and you won't have any clubhead speed, just arm speed. The result? All your shots will go the same length.

To prevent this: Start your hands and arms down; and *then* let your body turn forward. This motion will keep your arms and body connected. If you start your downswing with your body instead of your hands and arms, you will never have a connected golf swing.

5. Let your forearms rotate forward. When you hit the ball, keep your head down until your arms have travelled past your head.

Sandra's Tip: If your shots tend to go right, this means

1. your clubface is *open* (*see* Glossary) when you hit the ball, instead of square to the target; and

2. you're hanging on to the club too tightly, which prevents your forearms from rotating soon enough. If this is happening, try to get the toe of the club in the air *earlier* on the forward swing.

And if your shots tend to go left, this means

1. your clubface is *closed* (*see* Glossary) when you hit the ball, instead of square to the target; and

2. your forearms are rotating too soon. If this is happening, try to slow down the release process (uncocking your wrists) during your downswing.

And if this sounds complicated, think of it like this: you're just trying to create some clubhead speed at impact

6

7

(impact is the moment the clubhead meets the ball) *and* keep the clubface square to the target so that the ball will go straight.

6. and 7. Finish in balance, with your weight on your front foot, your hands high, and your hips and shoulders facing the target.

Sandra's Tip: I know this all sounds very complicated! You're probably thinking, How am I going to learn all these positions and then let them happen naturally? Well, take a tip from the pros: Take it one step at a time. Don't succumb to paralysis by analysis. When the best players in the world stand over their shots, they have only one swing thought.

presumably gone. Accomplishing anything close to this is a distant dream for me, and I know it. Merely extending my swing beyond a parallel position (toe in the air, toe in the air) is more than enough to keep me fully occupied for the foreseeable future. I'm a minority of one, though; everyone else follows through nicely, even Janet, who arrived fifteen minutes late today and looks more frazzled than ever.

I've found a nice patch of soft earth to tee up in, and the ball isn't falling off the tee nearly so often. Suddenly Sandra is behind me, chuckling. "Why is it that beginners *always* tee up in a divot?" she says. She sees my blank face. "You call this gouge in the ground a divot, Loral. Somebody did that when they hit the ground with a golf club. There's nothing wrong with taking a divot, but *you* need all the help you can get. Tee up the ball nice and high, and give yourself a decent lie. That divot was a quarter-inch deep." She pulls my neatly teed-up ball and tee out of the ground and puts them on a pristine patch of green grass. Now why would she do this? The minute I hit the ball I promptly tear up that lovely grass! I step forward to retrieve the huge piece of grass and turf I've gouged out. Sandra grabs me from behind in something akin to a football tackle. "Leave it!" she shrieks.

"But . . . !" I splutter, adding sanctimoniously, "I thought you were supposed to replace your divots."

"Not on the practice range!" Sandra replies. "I don't want you getting hit by a ball. You never know what direction a student's ball is going to take.

"This is golf grass," she continues. "You mustn't be afraid to mess it up. You're *supposed* to brush the grass every time you make a practice swing, and if you take a divot, that's okay."

I realize I must bone up on strange new words like *divot*. Sandra is hip to this and makes a joke of it: "Yes, I'm bilingual: I speak English and I speak golf. Have you ever noticed that when you enter a roomful of golfers, it sounds like another language?" Tell me about it! All those warm summer nights in the backyard, tuning out endless golf talk between David and his cronies.

Sandra is determined to initiate us thoroughly. "When you miss a ball like Loral just did . . . what's it called?" she asks.

"Missing a ball," I reply stupidly, sensing a trick question. Not so.

"A whiff," Sandra replies. A term I'd better get used to fast. "Now," Sandra continues, not missing a beat, "will Loral lose a stroke if she swings at the ball and completely misses it?"

"No," Terry replies. She is a forgiving soul.

"Wrong!" Sandra says. "Loral will certainly lose a stroke." Well, fine and dandy,

---

SANDRA'S TIP

When you start playing golf, your shots will all travel much the same distance, no matter which club you use. Try not to get discouraged. Keep practising, and soon your distance will increase.

Sandra, I think to myself. But what about that conversation I had with an American friend last week about President Clinton and his "mulligans"? My friend, an avid golfer who considers himself scrupulously honest, was pooh-poohing Clinton's alleged score, citing "all those mulligans he didn't count." "Mulligans," he had explained patiently, are bad shots or missed shots that you just conveniently forget about. "Taking mulligans" sounds like my kind of game. But Sandra, it seems, is a purist.

And she's on a roll. "Yes, Loral loses a stroke. And the book of rules for golf is *this* thick. But the thing to remember when you're a beginner is not to get hung up on *some* rules. Rules such as: Whoever is farthest away from the hole must hit first. Play through. Don't hold up play. Sink your putt, even if it takes four, five strokes – and move on. We call this 'Ready Golf.'

"When my husband, John, and I play, we try to get the first tee-off time. We play a round in two, two and a half, hours. Which means, since we tee off at 6:30 or 7 A.M., that we're finished by 9 or 9:30. Then we have breakfast and get on with our day. I'd go *brain-dead* if every game of golf took up my entire day . . . four to five hours, plus forty-five minutes to an hour each way getting there and home. Who has the time? Speed up your play. Get on with your game and get on with your life."

She spends a few minutes talking about how golf is different for women – harder in many ways than it is for men. "For one thing," she says, "men often hack away on the course and get away with it, because they have the strength to hit the ball hard, even if it goes into the trees. We can't do this because we simply do not have the muscle power. So, we don't have a choice: we have to learn how to do it right." I'm impressed with the way she includes herself in a chummy, unpretentious sort of way. She makes it sound as if she's just any old woman player. So far she hasn't made a single reference to her stellar career on the LPGA Tour. And no name-dropping – no references to "my friend Nancy Lopez," or whatever.

"The statistics tell us that 52 per cent of people taking up golf are women, but that 50 per cent of those women give it up in the first year," Sandra goes on. "Well, I just don't believe this! What I see all the time in my golf clinics and with my individual students are women who don't give up golf – they just put golf on the back burner, because they're so busy – with the house, the kids, the mortgage, just keeping it all going and performing that juggling act we women are so well-known for.

"Janet, you're a good example of what I'm talking about. You rush in here late, you rush out early. You're helping Joe in the office, the kids are at home . . ." Janet nods her head in agreement, ponytail bobbing. "Now, the women who do *not* put golf on the back burner are the career executives," Sandra continues. "These women are on the move. They attack golf the way they do their careers, because they have to keep up with their male colleagues on the golf course as well as in the office. These women come to me for lessons, too. But they usually arrange private lessons, because they can't clear a space for a clinic, three days in a row."

As I say to Sharon on the way home, Sandra seems to me a true feminist in all the best senses of the word. She tirelessly promotes *women* and golf. She never communicates any sense of separation between us, the poor benighted duffers (a word Sandra never uses), and her, the brilliant pro. I admire her empathy with homemakers who are taking up golf to enjoy it with their husbands. It's clear she has great respect for them and the fraught lives they lead, and their attempts to carve out a little space for themselves through golf. She herself has never been a traditional homemaker – she has no children and has worked all her life – but she includes homemakers in her pantheon of women.

Sharon is a bit discouraged. She didn't do so spectacularly today, she sighs: "But that's golf! Just when you think you've improved, it gets the better of you again."

The weather forecast on the morning of Lesson Three is ominous: high winds up to a hundred kilometres an hour and the temperature dropping like a stone. Whatever will it be like at the Golf Ranch, where winds on a normal spring day are no joke? But I'm too proud to call Sandra before setting out. "If you want to be a golfer, you have to be an optimist," she said yesterday when somebody complained about the wind. "This would be considered a fine summer's day in Scotland!" No, I don't want Sandra to think I'm a golf wimp, a soft city slicker. Besides, if she'd decided to cancel the class, surely she'd have telephoned us.

The drive out is harrowing, trash flying across the highway, wind buffeting the car, skies to the north menacingly black. We arrive to find Sandra sitting in the parking lot in her vanity-plated British-racing-green Blazer, talking on her car phone. She climbs out in a Gore-Tex rainsuit and shouts into the wind, "9:30 on Monday." What? we ask. "The others have come and gone. The class is cancelled.

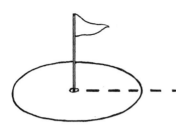

4. ALIGNMENT

Alignment means lining up or aligning your body, clubhead, and ball properly so that you can hit the ball on target.

1. Line up your ball and clubhead to the target.

2. Line up your body parallel to the target line. Your shoulders, arms, hips, knees, and feet are all on the same line – to the *left* of the target.

Sandra's Tip: Align your clubhead first, then your body. If you do it backwards – align your body, then your clubhead – your ball and clubhead will always be to the right of the target.

Your target is a long way away. So pick an object about six inches in front of you that is in line with your target. A divot, a flower, a piece of clover will do. Choose something that is natural (you can't put something there!).

Ball Position: If you are using a short iron (a 9- or 8-iron), the ball should be in the centre of your stance. As your clubs get longer, the ball should move towards your left foot. With the longest club (the driver), you play the ball off your left heel.

Sandra's Tip: When hitting irons, place the ball towards the centre or centre front in your stance. When playing your woods, favour a ball position off your left heel. This allows the ball to be hit with a sweeping motion with your woods, and a downward motion for your irons.

You can't even stand up out there!" she says, pointing in the direction of the practice range. "Think about what you've learned over the weekend. See you Monday."

The drive back is just as horrendous, but I secretly welcome this unexpected breather in my crash introduction to golf. A chance to rest my stiff muscles – and not look at a golf club for four days.

On Monday morning the weather is only marginally better. Temperatures in the low teens and sixty-kilometre winds predicted. Sandra comes to class in a spiffy gold-trimmed black jacket, snug-fitting corduroy pants, two turtlenecks, black visor – everything beautifully colour-coordinated. I've resorted to my ancient but exceptionally warm down vest over a thick turtleneck sweater and windbreaker. I'm so bulked up I can barely swing my arms.

Today, Sandra teaches the fourth, and last, Golf Basic: Alignment.

"Okay, ladies, let's get started," she says, stepping into the teeth of the wind, as Terry, Sharon, and I try not to shiver. Janet isn't here: she couldn't rearrange her tight schedule to accommodate the change in time. "As of today," Sandra continues, "you're not hitting just anywhere. Now you have to aim for a target."

She lays a golf club on the ground in front of her, pointing towards a yellow flag a hundred yards or so out on the practice range. Then she places a tee a few inches in front of the club. "This is what Jack Nicklaus always does," she explains. "Obviously, he can't put a tee in the ground the way I have, but what he does is line up his clubface with a blade of grass or a flower or a piece of clover or whatever, about six inches in front of him, aligned with his target.

"The most common mistake golfers make when they try to align their ball to the target is aligning their *body* to the target, instead of the clubface," Sandra continues. "They line up their body to the target like this" – Sandra stands parallel to her club – "and then they put their clubhead down, like this. Sharon, where am I lined up now?"

"To the right of the target," Sharon replies.

"Right! You see, if you do it that way, your ball and your clubhead will always be to the right of the target.

"So, align your clubhead *first* and then your body. The clubhead is on target and your body is slightly to the *left* of the target."

We all practise alignment for a few minutes. "Don't worry too much about alignment for the moment," Sandra tells me quietly: I need to work on my swing for now. Specifically, my balance and that dratted wristcock, which I simply cannot seem to master.

Balance, of course, is all about keeping my feet still. I try a new tip from Sandra: bending my knees ever so slightly towards each other "as if holding a volleyball between your legs. Then, when you swing, concentrate on not dropping the ball." This is an image I can visualize. I find it helps me keep grounded.

The good news is that, for the first time during the three lessons, it's all starting to feel not quite so complicated. I feel almost as if it's beginning to come together and become comprehensible . . . even doable. Is it possible I'm starting to get it?

And then, *voilà*! Sandra is standing out there on the range, wind still smartly whipping around us all, with a video camera on her shoulder. She tapes each of us going through the full swing, then invites us into her little teaching shed to show us what she's recorded. I'm pleasantly surprised by what I see. At least one of the swings on the video looks . . . well, it looks okay. Sandra gives me some nice strokes, telling me I look as if I know what I'm doing. Then she slows down the tape and shows me how my hand isn't *quite* facing forward the way it should and, hence, the ball didn't go quite where it should have. But heck, it got off the ground! And, amazingly, on the follow-through my right arm is nicely extended, something women have a particularly hard time doing because, as Sandra has said, we tend to pull our arms close to our bodies.

Sharon is doing fine. She executes her swing very slowly and deliberately and, Sandra tells her, she has excellent *tempo*, a word she hasn't unleashed on us before. Sharon's well-tempered tempo I do *not* have. This surprises Sandra a little, she says. She had "read" me as a slower, more deliberate, type. I'm proving to be quite the opposite: I have a quick, jerky swing. I have no rhythm – and my tempo is off. Sounds like a bad rock band. But Sandra, ever the optimist, puts a positive spin on all this: "*I* think you're getting too quick because you're so keen! Look at your cousin!" she says to Sharon. "She's raring to go. It's sheer enthusiasm that's making her go so fast." Sharon nods in agreement. Could Sandra be right? I hadn't thought of myself as enthusiastic, exactly, yet. But maybe . . .

To wrap up the class, Sandra tells each of us to try using a wood. "Grip down on the club a bit if it feels awkward," she instructs. Which I do: it feels *very* long. But the minute I pick the wood up, I love the feel of it. To my surprise, it seems much lighter than the iron. And I like its big fat head! It has a nice heft to it. Irons, in comparison, look sort of mean and meagre. And woods look like great big fun toys. I decide I'm a wood person.

This is predictable, Sandra says: beginners are either iron people or wood people. Sharon is an iron person. Why? I ask her. Well, Sharon replies thoughtfully, "I guess it's because I use them much more than my woods. You use a wood to tee off with. But on the fairway, you almost always use irons."

As our clinic draws to a close, Sandra reminds us all to practise what we've learned. "If you go away from a beginners' clinic and don't practise for a week, you'll forget everything you've been taught," she says. "That's why I give these clinics three days in a row: to reinforce what you learn right away."

"Well, Sharon," I ask as we drive home, "when are you going out to practise?"

"Oh, Richard and I are going to play next weekend at our club – if it's not twenty below, that is," Sharon answers. "So I'll try to get in some practice on the range before we play our round."

I know it's much more important that *I* practise right away, since everything Sandra packed into the clinic was totally new to me. The only thing I'm sure I won't forget is that I'm no golf natural: I know I'm going to have to work at this if I'm going to get anywhere. But alas, alack, I'm suddenly bunkered by life: specifically my stepson's wedding. David has already left with a vanload of relatives for St. Louis, Missouri, the bride's home, and I am following him by air in a couple of days. It will be at least ten days, maybe more, until I retackle golf. If Sandra says you forget everything in a week, I fear I'll return a golf-clean slate.

CHAPTER 4

GOLF IS A GAME OF ADJUSTMENTS

It's the middle of May and the ferocious weather continues. While we were away at Shane and Stephanie's wedding there were torrential rains, high winds, and near-freezing temperatures. In the three days since we've returned, David and a cousin who is visiting post-wedding attempted a golf game at a course just north of the Golf Ranch. It was besieged by gale-force winds. They had lunch and fled. Yesterday, when I stopped for gas just north of Toronto on my way back from visiting my parents in Parry Sound, the winds threatened to flatten the gas jockey and me. "Winter's back!" he screamed, his voice trailing off into a sudden blast. So this morning, the day I have arranged to "audit" another beginners' clinic at the Ranch, I screw my courage to the sticking place, as Lady Macbeth counselled, and telephone Sandra. "I know I'm supposed to be an optimist," I say, "but are you really going to be out there today?"

"Just call us Canada Post!" Sandra sings into the receiver. "Rain, snow, sleet, hail . . . we just carry on!"

I'd hoped for an out. It's the beginning of a long weekend, the first one of the "summer," when all of urban Ontario drives north like lemmings running to the sea "to open up the cottage." I anticipate highway gridlock as well as wind and weather. And besides, I'm not in a golf mood. I haven't had a single one of Sandra's so-called "swing thoughts" for ten days now and, frankly, I feel much better for it.

I arrive to find Sandra sitting in the parking lot in her Blazer van, wearing her Gore-Tex Meet-Me-in-Patagonia snowsuit. "Oh hello, Loral," she squeaks out the window. She's sucking a lozenge.

"Have you caught a cold from all this godawful weather?" I ask.

"No," she croaks, "I've just lost my voice from teaching all the time. And tomorrow morning at seven," she swallows the lozenge, "I'm hosting a one-hour radio show . . . *live*. I'm sitting in for Tim O'Connor on the 'Bell Canada Golf Hour.' I've never *done* a one-hour radio program. And sounding like *this* . . ." The squeak trails off into the howl of the wind.

Even reading names out of a phone book on live radio would rank as the mother-of-all-terrors for *me*. But, before I can crank out a single word of empathy, the familiar Sandra – self-confident, bouncy, enthusiastic – is back. Her face crinkles into one of her irresistible smiles and she recites the "incredible" line-up of items and interviews she's cobbled together. She even has a token male, she crows, just the ticket for those golf shows with their standard token female!

"That reminds me," she says, leaning over to the passenger seat to pick something up. She hands me a glossy magazine with Michelle McGann, the stylish young American golfer, on the cover. "It's my new magazine, *World of Women's Golf!*" she says. "Premiere issue." Her face is aglow. She thrusts it into my hand.

Sandra looks at her watch. Time to get going. She pulls on a thick woollen toque, climbs out of the van, and trots over to her teaching area, all high spirits and energy once more. I've brought a large thermometer I borrowed from our back deck as I left the house this morning. If I'm going to suffer this arctic golf madness, I want to record it for my grandchildren: *Do you have any idea what a hard life your grandmother endured? Why, she braved ice, torrent, and gale – and all for golf.* The thermometer registers 10°C in the lee of the teaching shed. That would put the wind chill around zero.

I'm crashing the third class of a beginners' clinic. It's full – five women not counting me – and four of the five are Women Like Me (WLM), mid-forties to mid-fifties, comfortable figures that probably mirror their incomes, almost surely married, well dressed but a long way from chic. The fifth woman is different: she's leggy, black-haired, and beautiful, and she's wearing a stylish ski jacket, trendy wraparound dark glasses, and black tights that make her look even slimmer and leggier than she is. She's not a day over thirty. She came alone, last, and she stands ever so slightly apart from our cosy group of lumpen matrons.

We start with the warming-up exercises. I get the same one – the one with the club across the shoulders, where I tilt towards the non-existent ball with alternating shoulders – utterly wrong, again. "No, Loral, weight on your *other* left foot." Yeah, Sandra.

We get out and start swinging and I'm hopeless. The ball dribbles along the ground, or hooks to the left. Everything feels terrible: my shoulders, my back, even the weight of the club in my hands. I don't want to be doing this. I feel slightly sick to my stomach. I want to go home. Sandra goes down the line, encouraging and correcting – and ignores me. So this is what it's going to be like now, I sulk. We have this deal where I audit her clinics according to my own pace, and she's going to treat me as if I weren't here. I curse silently, and then out loud, as I continue to hit my pathetic balls. No one takes any notice.

Meanwhile, the Beauty, who is in front of me, is swinging with stunning grace. She's hitting the ball with a perfect arc and good distance. Sandra tells us all to watch her. She is beautiful to watch. She's loose, she swings way back on the backswing, her torso swivels like a supple pretzel. Damn.

Sandra stands back and lectures. "I want you to take home one swing thought from this clinic," she says. "Bend your shoulder to the ball and hitchhike those thumbs!" She pounds her point home. We all start swinging again. I try to concentrate on Sandra's swing thought, and also on keeping my left foot on the ground while I go through the backswing. I remember her tip about holding a volleyball between my knees. This seems to help me keep my feet grounded.

I am aware of what my feet are doing today. This is a first. For some reason, it no longer seems a problem. Before, I couldn't concentrate on my feet no matter how hard I tried. Does this mean I've progressed? My yoga teacher tells me awareness is everything. Awareness or no, I *cannot* get the ball off the ground. It hugs the earth, and shoots off to the left. I have no idea what I'm doing wrong – and Sandra is ignoring me.

Sandra tells us to take a break again. This time she talks about the importance of keeping loose, and of keeping your arms straight as you follow through ("the backs of the hands form a mirror image: back of the left hand faces forward at the top of the backswing, back of the right hand faces forward on the follow-through").

Keep the arms straight. And get loose, I tell myself. And don't forget to keep it smooth. I keep on swinging. And then, I do it. And I do it again. And one or two more times. "Hey, Loral, okay!" Sandra says quietly. I beam: she noticed me! Then I think to myself, What a baby I am! I can't bear it when "Teach" ignores me and now just look at me, will ya, when she gives me some strokes. I'm behaving like a two-year-old. "Are you back, Loral?" Sandra says. Yeah, Sandra, I'm back.

Later, Sandra explains what she did: she knew I'd been away for ten days; she knew I would be tight. So she just let me swing for half an hour or so until I loosened up and my swing, such as it is, came back. "That's the way it goes, Loral. Mollycoddling you wouldn't help you. You gotta do it yourself!"

Inside the teaching shack, she shows us videos of our swings. She uses the Beauty, a young lawyer, I learn, as our model. "Let's face it, ladies," Sandra says, "she's got a few years on the rest of us. She's much looser; she can swing much more freely. And look at that torque!" Sandra points at her long, lithe torso as she turns through the swing. "It reminds me of Tiger Woods' torque," Sandra adds, cautioning the Beauty not to take this *too* literally. But Sandra is right. It really is reminiscent of that beautiful torque-cum-twist that Tiger performs with every swing. I'm wildly envious.

The Beauty takes all this gracefully. "Whoever it was that taught you that swing did a good job," Sandra says.

"Well, I dumped him," says the Beauty.

"Think of it this way: He gave good value!" says Sandra.

On Saturday and Sunday, I hang in for Lessons Two and Three of another beginners' clinic. This one is made up of young career women taking advantage of the long weekend to cram in Sandra's three-day package. Their youth notwithstanding, they're no match for the Beauty. In fact, four of the five remind me of myself during my first clinic. They're really struggling – with basics like grip, posture, arm extension, wristcock, balance. Sandra puts their problems down to "paralysis by analysis," her expression for golfers who think too much instead of just relaxing and letting it happen. Well, what to expect, she says, from highly educated, cerebral women like you? There's a banker, a lawyer, a telecommunications consultant, and a psychotherapist in this group.

Sandra turns to the fifth woman. "Now, you're different, Karen," she says. Karen looks like a shampoo commercial. Her freckled face is make-up-free and looks freshly scrubbed, and she has a mass of shining golden-brown hair that cascades over the collar of her bulky jacket. She could be sixteen. She's not. "In every one of my clinics, there's always one person who's a natural," Sandra says. "And you're it, Karen." The rest of us have been enviously eyeing Karen's easy, loose swing. She just stands up to the ball and lets it fly. "So what do *you* do for a living?" Sandra asks.

"Oh," Karen shrugs, "I'm a dermatologist." Sandra is stunned. This easygoing, fresh-faced young woman who has absorbed the rhythms of the golf swing like a blotter has endured the rigours of medical school? From the look on Sandra's face, I would guess she had imagined Karen as, maybe, a waterskiing instructor. Karen laughs. "Believe it or not, I'm a classic Type-A personality. And my friends didn't think I'd be any good at all at golf – for precisely that reason. So," Karen grins mischievously, "I just decided I would prove everybody wrong and *be loose!*" And loose she is. Analysis without paralysis, perhaps? Sandra can add that one to her golf lexicon.

Apart from Karen – and, hey, who can compete with the clinic natural? – I'm one of the better students in the class! No small achievement, considering the fact I'm ten to twenty years older than every one of them. I instruct my self-confidence to take a baby step forward, and it works the first time I test it. Sandra puts us through a drill she hasn't used in the other clinics I've attended. She decides she's going to make us perform for each other, in order to get used to teeing off in front of strangers. "Teeing off at the first tee is always the most intimidating moment of a golf game," she says. "Chances are other people are watching you, and you're going to feel nervous and self-conscious." Surprise, surprise. I stand up in front of these young, successful women and hit a very decent ball. Sandra takes a look at my shot and says, "Oh well, *she's* had more lessons than the rest of you."

Sandra is curious about what David thinks about my golf progress. "Has he seen your swing yet?" she asks. Well, no, in fact. But the next day is Sunday, and David decides to drive out to the Golf Ranch with me, buy a bucket of balls during the clinic, and then let me show him my swing. Which he does. He stands well back, trying to be unobtrusive, while I swing away. Sandra stands back with him, chatting, while I do my best to keep cool.

Later, as we drive away, I pump David for the details of their conversation. "She says you set up well," David reports, and that that's what she emphasizes in her beginners' clinics: the importance of a good grip, stance, posture, and alignment. "She says that your swing can be fine-tuned later," he goes on. "That's something that you'll be working on *ad infinitum*. But the basic set-up is something that *must* come as second nature to you."

Over lunch, I recount how Sandra told the class today that golf is a game of adjustments, unlike, say, tennis, where you always use the same racket against your opponent. "In golf," she said, "you're constantly choosing which club to use, analysing the terrain, the slopes, the distances. This is the challenge of golf – and why you never stop learning." And she included herself in this process, I add. "She says *she* never stops learning."

I sip at my Bloody Caesar. "Maybe *Sandra* never stops learning," I continue. "I mean, she knows so much about the game and she's at a level where, I suppose, every tiny adjustment matters. But *me*? I can see myself going around a golf course just blindly hitting the ball, trying to get from A to B. I'm sure there's lots to think about if you know a lot, but, when you're a beginner, aren't you more likely just to let it all wash over you? Couldn't it be fairly mindless? Does *everyone* who golfs consider it a deep-thinking game?"

David is silent for a minute. "You know," he answers, "the wonderful thing about golf is that *every hole is a different drama.* You never play the same shot twice. That's what Sandra meant when she said, 'Golf is a game of adjustments.' Choosing which club you're going to use is the least of it. Every single time you play a game – and this is no different if you play the same course over and over and over again – *every shot is different.* You never find yourself in exactly the same lie, with the temperature exactly the same, the wind, the sun, the clouds the same, the wetness or the dryness of the grass, the length of the grass, the position of your playing partner . . . There is no such thing as an identical golf shot."

Well. I take a few moments to digest all this. What David has just described sounds an awful lot like "mindfulness" – another of those yoga ideals that I find difficult to master. Mindfulness means being totally present in the moment, full awareness of the here and now. Whereas *my* mind has an amazing capacity for going blank. I really wonder if I'm going to find this game endlessly changeable and fascinating. As Dianne pointed out when we were watching the Masters, for every hole to become a different drama you really have to *concentrate.* Otherwise, there's a terrible sameness to it all, is there not?

CHAPTER 5

THE SHORT GAME

"I can see myself getting excited about learning how to hit the ball with that marvellous firecracker sound Andy makes when he hits the ball a ton," I said to Dianne last March when I was debating whether to give golf a try. "But *putting*? I mean, how can anyone get interested in that?"

"For heaven's sake, don't worry about it right now, Loral," Dianne replied with her usual matter-of-factness. "Get a grip on the full swing first. It took me at least two years before I paid any attention to putting. I only started taking it seriously when I finally realized how important it is."

I'm going to try putting for the first time tomorrow when Sandra starts her short-game clinics for the season. But the importance of putting has been pounded into my head for some time. The golf pooh-bahs made much about Tiger Woods winning the Masters because he had a "complete game," meaning his

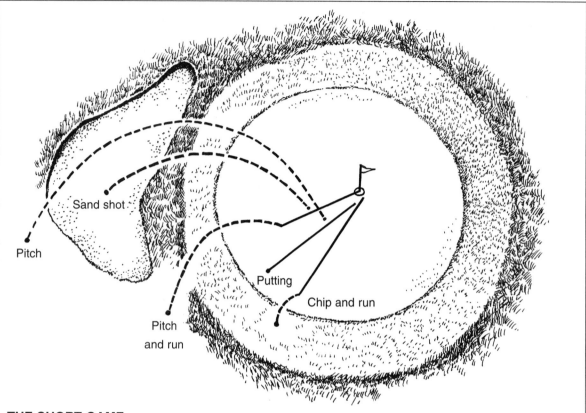

Sand shot

Pitch

Putting

Chip and run

Pitch
and run

THE SHORT GAME

The short game refers to all the shots you make around the green. It is a game unto itself. The short game includes putting, chipping, pitching, and sand play. Together these make up 65 per cent of your score. New golfers like to practise their long game. But if you really want to reduce your score, you should spend more time practising your short game.

short game was just as solid as his long hitting. And David has lectured me *ad nauseam* about the Importance of the Short Game. "Figure it out for yourself," he instructs. "To par a hole, you're expected to two-putt – in other words, not putt more than two times on the green before you hole the ball. Two times eighteen holes is thirty-six. That's half of seventy-two, which is par for the average golf course. So half your score comes from putting.

"Once you start playing real games, you'll realize very fast that you'll *never* get your scores down until you learn how to putt half-decently. Remember the cliché: You drive for show and putt for dough."

Sandra teaches the short game at a municipal golf course southwest of Toronto, near her hometown of Oakville. She gives three-day clinics, an hour and a quarter each, just like her long-game clinics. I'm looking forward to a break from focusing on the full swing. Not that I have the foggiest idea what the short-game clinic entails. With any luck, she'll explain those odd terms "chipping" and "pitching," as well as putting – if, indeed, there's anything to teach about putting. Surely, putting is easy – relaxing, for a change. And I'm looking forward to seeing a real golf course. This one is an "executive" course, which means, apparently, a short course, with mostly par-3 holes. But the name intrigues me: I can't help fantasizing that I'm going to some sort of corporate course where I'll meet men in suits.

The Oakville Executive Golf Course comes as a bit of a surprise, just beyond a steep hill on a winding country road. The setting is much more pastoral and protected than the Golf Ranch, but, alas, a cold wind has found it on what is otherwise a bright, sunny day. When I arrive, Sandra and her husband, John McDermid, are setting up for the lesson beside a large practice putting green in front of a small, pretty clubhouse with a view of the Niagara Escarpment.

There are thirteen women in the class, including me. I'm a bit taken aback by the number, after the intimate four- to six-student full-swing clinics. But John is teaching the class with Sandra, so the student-teacher ratio is the same.

Sandra begins with a short talk about choosing a putter. Putters aren't included with a standard set of golf clubs, she says. You buy a putter separately – and choosing a putter is a very personal decision. Already I sense a difference in approach. In the full-swing clinic, she talked about choosing clubs that are the right size and flexibility for each individual's height, build, and strength. Personal taste did not enter the discussion.

As the class unfolds, this theme continues. "When you putt, you don't hit the ball, you *stroke* it," Sandra says. "Putting is all about *feel.*" She demonstrates with three or four beautiful putts – right into the hole – which she performs with a careless grace. A large part of putting accurately is about learning how to "read" a green to determine which way it "breaks," she continues. She demonstrates once again. "This putt should break to the right, just about here . . . at the top of this ridge," she says. And it does, precisely where she says it will. Gosh.

SANDRA'S TEACHING TIP

HOW TO READ A GREEN

"Reading" the green means deciding which way the ball is going to roll after you have stroked it. You can gauge this from determining the slope of the green and the "grain" of the grass. The slope usually is fairly easy to see: You look at the green between the ball and the hole to see which side is higher. The ball will "break" to the low side, which means you should aim for the high side.

"Grain" means the angle at which the grass is growing. When grass looks shiny and smooth, it usually is faster and you will be "going with the grain." If the grass looks dull, it usually is slower and you will be going against the grain.

Look, but don't touch: You determine the grain of the green by looking at it closely. You cannot use your putter or your hand to test the grain. If you do, there is a two-stroke penalty.

And remember: The speed of the green is more important to your putt than the break of the green. Your touch when you stroke the ball is the most important part of your putt.

Sandra's Tip: If you arrive at the golf course with a few minutes to spare before tee-off time, go to the practice green and acquaint yourself with the speed of the greens you are about to play. This will help you build the confidence you need for putting, as well as eliminate guesswork on the first green.

Putting is also about accuracy, of course. A nanomillimetre here, a nanomillimetre there makes all the difference, I imagine David would say. One inviolable rule for accurate putting, Sandra and John say, is standing so that your eyes are directly over the ball. They ask us to place a ball on the ground and then drop another ball from eye level, directly below our sight line. If the dropped ball hits the ball on the ground, your eyes are positioned correctly. Another important rule is proper alignment. "Always take time to line up your ball to the hole," Sandra says. "This takes an extra couple of seconds, but it's worth it." This is the only time in the entire game of golf that you're allowed to touch the ball while it's in play, she explains. And you are allowed to do so only if you mark its position first, *before* you pick it up.

SANDRA EXPLAINS IMPORTANT RULES ON THE GREEN

• You may remove any loose "impediments" on the green, such as leaves, twigs, pine cones, or sand. But be careful to clear away debris such as loose sand from a bunker with the *back* of your hand. If you use the palm of your hand, you can be accused of "testing the green," and incur a two-stroke penalty.

• *Before* you pick up your ball you must "mark" its position on the green. You do this by placing a coin or ball marker directly *behind* the ball. (Loral kept getting this reversed and marking *in front* of the ball. Wrong!) Now you can pick up your ball. When you're ready to play, put the ball back down as close as possible to its original position. Once you understand this sequence, you can go through it very fast in order to maintain the rhythm of play.

The Four Basics Sandra considers so essential to learning the full swing are not nearly so rigid when it comes to putting. For example, the V shape of the arms, essential to proper set-up for the full swing, is not necessary. When you putt, your arms are much more relaxed-looking – elbows slightly bent, held close to the body.

You can even get a bit creative with your putting grip. The veteran LPGA star Nancy Lopez uses a Reverse Overlapping Grip, Sandra says, but extends her index finger down the shaft of the putter. This little idiosyncrasy makes it easier for her to keep the putter steady. Another alternative is the Cross-Handed Grip – basically the Overlapping Grip upside down, reversing the position of the left and right hands. Which one to choose? Whichever grip helps you keep the putter absolutely steady seems to be what's important. I pick the Cross-Handed Grip; it feels a bit strange, but it seems to do the job.

As for putting posture and stance, once again the important thing is to be relaxed and balanced. Sandra stands a bit pigeon-toed, she tells us, "a habit I developed when I was on the Tour, because it made me feel secure." But pigeon-toed isn't the "correct" stance; it's a choice.

All of which seems pretty straightforward, and refreshingly flexible. But *nothing* is going well for me today. In a word, I feel terrible. I'm cold, and every joint and muscle is aching. And I was so looking forward to this brand-new part of the game! By the end of the clinic I'm so chilled I find it impossible to concentrate. I

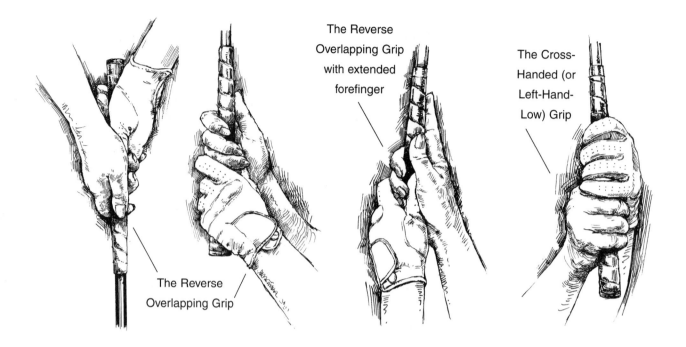

The Reverse Overlapping Grip with extended forefinger

The Cross-Handed (or Left-Hand-Low) Grip

The Reverse Overlapping Grip

1. PUTTING

The Putting Grip

Most golfers change their grip when they putt. The handle, also known as the grip, of a putter invites a different grip because it's triangular, rather than round like the rest of your clubs. The two most popular putting grips are the Reverse Overlapping Grip and the Cross-Handed, or Left-Hand-Low, Grip.

The Reverse Overlapping Grip

Take hold of the grip with your right hand. Now place your left hand above it (closer to the top end of the grip) on the shaft with your left forefinger on top and between your baby and ring finger on your right hand. Your thumbs are straight down the shaft. Some golfers like to extend the forefinger of their right hand down the shaft as well, for better stability. Nancy Lopez, one of golf's all-time best players, as well as a superb putter, does this.

The Cross-Handed (or Left-Hand-Low) Grip

Place your left hand below your right hand with your thumbs straight down the shaft. The baby finger of your left hand sits between and on top of the forefinger and middle finger of your right hand. Golf pros Tom Kite, Fred Couples, Kelly Robbins, and Jim Furyk use this grip.

Sandra's Tip: Regardless of which putting grip you choose, your palms always face each other. And try to relax your hands, arms, and shoulders, so that you develop a sense of feel when you putt.

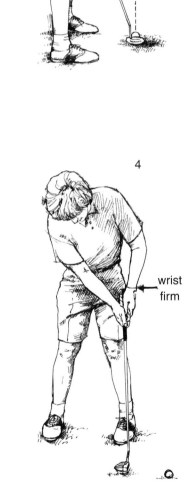

wrist firm

Putting Basics

1. *The Posture:* Bend from your hips, as you do for the full swing.

The Stance: The width of your stance is up to you. But as a guideline, place your feet comfortably, about the same distance apart as your shoulders. Distribute your weight evenly or, if you wish, favour your left foot slightly. *Never* put your weight on your right (back) foot.

Keep Your Body Still: Do not move your head to see where the ball is going. With short putts, listen for the putt to fall into the hole.

Ball Position: Position the ball towards your left (front) foot.

2. Before you make your putt, make sure your eyes are directly over the ball.

3. and 4. Keep your putter low, close to the green, during your back and forward stroke.

Ideally your putter goes back the same distance as it comes through. However, it's easy to decelerate when you putt instead of *accelerating* through the ball as you should. To prevent this, think of your stroke as 40 per cent backstroke and 60 per cent forward stroke. *Smooth acceleration is extremely important in the short game.*

And remember to stroke the ball; do *not* hit it!

Stroking versus Hitting

The putting stroke allows the shoulders, arms, hands, and putter to move at the same speed. The angle set by the left wrist should not change. Many people *hit* their putts. If you do that, your right hand passes the left hand. When this happens, you never develop a sense of feel for distance. When you hit a putt, the clubhead explodes into the ball, causing inconsistent distance control. You should *stroke* your putt.

SANDRA'S TEACHING TIP

HOW TO LINE UP YOUR PUTT

Mark your ball, then pick it up and put it down again with the brand name in line with the direction of your putt. Now place your putter head flat on the green with the name (and aim) of your ball continuing through the straight line that is marked through the sweet spot of your putter. The face of your putter now is square to your target.

If your putter does not have a dot or line on the top edge indicating its sweet spot, ask a pro or an experienced golfer to help you find it. Then draw a line on your putter to help you align your ball. Your putt will hit more solidly from the sweet spot.

---

bolt into the clubhouse and rapidly down two cups of coffee, desperately trying to warm myself up from the inside out. Teeth chattering, bones aching, I drive the fifty-five kilometres home and collapse – exhausted and unable to relax at the same time. Is it the drive or the golf? Whichever, my body is a wreck.

The weather report the following morning is more of the same – fierce winds, a high of 12°C, an arctic front moving in that means three more weeks of cold, wet weather. Time to get a grip, "button down the hatches," as my son used to say as a little boy in moments of crisis. I don't own any Gore-Tex, but as a fifth-generation Canadian I do understand the concept of layering. I assemble my warmest outfit yet, starting with long underwear, then adding heavy corduroy pants, undershirt, woollen turtleneck, sweatshirt, all topped with my trusty down-filled vest.

The weather at Oakville Executive (where I have sighted no men in suits) is as nasty as ever, but I *am* warmer. I credit my long underwear. Why didn't I think of that before? Of course, Sandra is rosy-cheeked and Gore-Texed, sublimely oblivious to the arctic conditions. I concede defeat in the face of competition from a

SANDRA'S TIP

GOLFING IN COLD WEATHER

If you wait for a perfect day to play golf, you'll have a very short life as a golfer. The solution? Dress for the weather! Or have good outerwear ready in case of a change of weather.

In really cold weather, I start by making sure my head and hands are warm. I wear a toque or headband that covers my ears; and golf gloves (*two* of them!). Cold-weather golf gloves are warm but not bulky, so that you can still feel your club. Sometimes I also use handwarmers inside my gloves.

Loral has discovered two keys to keeping warm on the golf course: a warm vest that doesn't impede your swing and the concept of layering. There are many light, warm, water- and windproof vests available today. Fleece jackets and vests made of synthetic fibres combine lightness and tremendous warmth. When I layer, I start with cotton next to my skin: a cotton turtleneck and leotards under long pants.

sixth-generation Canadian who claims the intrepid Laura Secord as an ancestor.

Today, chipping and pitching – short shots around the green – are on the agenda. "Chipping is a no-brainer shot," Sandra begins. "Once you learn the basic stance, foot position, and arm motion, you'll find that the shot just happens." Pitching is much the same kind of shot as chipping, but it's a longer shot. And the ball spends more time in the air. The rule of thumb: Chipping is 25 per cent "loft" (in the air) and 75 per cent "run" (as in roll along the ground). Pitching is the opposite: 75 per cent loft and 25 per cent run. Sandra demonstrates a pitch that moves in a beautiful arc about twenty feet from fringe to green.

"Now, what is Sandra doing that's different from chipping?" John asks us. *Dunno* is the general response.

"Not far wrong, because 'nothing' is the answer," Sandra says. "You perform the shot exactly the same. Only difference is that, in pitching, you bring the club back farther. And your feet are a bit farther apart."

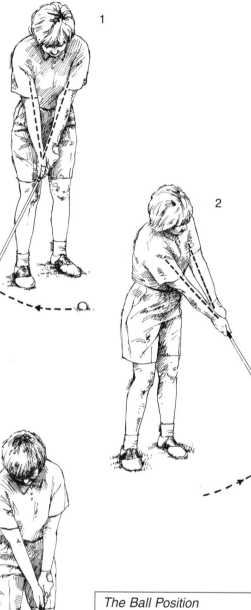

1

2

2. CHIPPING

Chipping is a short shot from the fringe (the slightly longer grass that encircles the green) onto the putting green. You use a 7- or 8-iron. When you chip, the ball travels about 25 per cent of the distance in the air and 75 per cent rolling on the green.

Chipping Basics

The Set-Up:

1. You use a narrow, open stance (*see* Glossary) with your right (back) foot closer to the ball than your left (front) foot.

Use whichever grip you use for the full swing. Grip down slightly lower on the shaft of your club, forming a V with your arms.

Come in close to the ball and place your weight so that you favour your left (front) foot slightly.

The chipping motion is straight back and straight forward, just like putting. Keep your wrists solid.

2. Take the club back and then accelerate smoothly the same distance forward.

Keep your body very, very still throughout your chipping shot.

Do not stand up and look at your shot. Trust me: If you maintain your posture and keep your left arm straight, you will get the ball in the air.

The Ball Position

The more forward your ball is (towards your left [front] foot), the more loft you will get on the ball. And the more you position your ball towards your right (back) foot, the lower the ball will travel and the more run the shot will have. *Note:* Leave your weight on your left (front) foot no matter where you position the ball.

So remember (right-handed players only): Left foot for loft, right foot for run.

Sandra's Tip: Chipping is *not* a difficult shot. Try to keep it simple.

3. PITCHING

When you move farther back from the green, you have to pitch the ball in the air and onto the green. When you pitch, the ball travels about 75 per cent of the distance in the air and runs 25 per cent of it on the green. You use a pitching wedge for this shot. It has a little more loft than a 7- or 8-iron, and it's a bit heavier.

Pitching Basics

The Set-Up:

1. You use an open stance, slightly wider than for chipping.

2. Stand fairly close to the ball. This will make it easier to get the ball in the air.

3. Leave more of your weight on your left (front) foot than your right.

4. Form a V with your arms.

5. Make sure your hands at address are slightly ahead of the ball.

6. Swing the club straight back, a little farther than you do when you chip.

7. Accelerate through the shot.

8. Maintain your posture. Do not stand up to watch where the shot goes.

9. For a lofty shot, play the ball off your left foot. For a pitch-and-run shot, play the ball towards your right foot. So it's still <u>l</u>eft for <u>l</u>oft, <u>r</u>ight for <u>r</u>un. But always leave more weight on your left (front) foot.

10. A pitching wedge has about forty-eight degrees of loft on it, which means that the club can easily get the ball in the air. Do *not* try to help the ball in the air by lifting it with the club. Hit *down* on the ball and let your pitching wedge do the work for you.

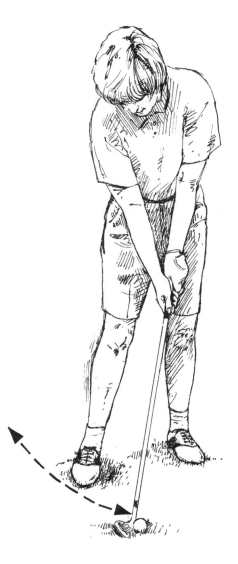

Chipping is *not* a no-brainer shot for me. Sandra instructs us to move our arms back and forth in a pendulum motion – without moving our bodies. Seems like an easy concept, but moving the arms straight back and straight forward like a ticking pendulum, *without moving the body at all*, looks much easier than it is. And the effort involved in keeping the arms straight without using the body or having the satisfaction of taking a good whack at the ball I find immensely unsatisfying. There's just no decent payoff with this shot! It's a piddly shot – a silly, nothing, penny-ante, who-gives-a-damn sort of shot. And I'm still aching all over.

"Don't forget to stand up and stretch out your back!" John keeps reminding us. "And shake out your hands after every few shots." Stiff and achy muscles are predictable for people of a certain age going through these small, exacting movements, John soothes. Alas, following his instructions makes no difference to *my* body. I'm a mess.

Pitching feels like a more serious shot: I can get a bit of heft into it. And I do better. I even get the ball nicely up into the air and down on the green several times in a row. But my chipping continues to be Class-A pathetic. I manage nothing beyond a longish putt, the ball rolling sadly along the ground.

On the drive home, I wonder if I've hit the wall, the golf wall. Can it be only two days since I was anticipating this so-called "short" game with high hopes? I thought it would be fun, relaxing, easier than the full swing. I imagined it would be like editing as opposed to writing. Writing is a raw process that has to come from the gut. Editing is more like fine-tuning, polishing, the illusion of perfecting. I thought putting and the short game would be like editing the full swing and the long game. A tiny, perfect closure. Not so. The whole game feels like a bunch of baloney.

"That's the way the game is," David says, when I bleat all this upon arriving home. "Hang in! Don't become one of the statistics." These are words to the wind. I am engulfed by a wave of emotional fragility.

I take a stroll through our back garden, beautiful and serene in the late-afternoon light. I love the long shadows and dappled sunlight of this time of day. I hear Domenic, our elderly Italian-Canadian neighbour, moving about quietly, inspecting his vegetables. Gardening is a satisfying way to enjoy summer, so much more productive than golf. I long to putter in *my* garden. That's what summer's all about – fragrant mucking about in the soil – not freezing one's butt on a windy green!

I lay these insights on David. "Remember what I told you about Tiger Woods when you said he was destined to win and win and win?" he replies. "I told you that golf is a game of nanomillimetres. The tiniest thing can interfere with your game."

"But what's happening to me is not tiny!" I pout. "This is major. I feel wretched and *nothing* is working. And, besides," I whine, "I'm not enjoying it."

"Now listen tight," David says. "*Everyone* goes through this – even Tiger Woods, although his 'wall' is legions away from yours. Just put your clubs down . . . until tomorrow. Things will start to click in again when you have a fresh start. You'll see."

I call Dianne. She's not home, so I pour my depression and desperation into her voicemail. She calls back early the next morning. As usual, she says all the right things. "Oh yes, Loral, I'm with you! I'm a fair-weather golfer, too. I don't like to play when it's cold *or* raining. And I can't stand wearing tons of clothes: it's *very* restricting.

"Of course, nothing stops *Andy* golfing," she goes on. "He's in Ireland for a couple of weeks right now with eight pals, having the time of his life. He took all kinds of cold-weather gear, including a full rainsuit, two pairs of golf shoes, lots of sweaters. And wouldn't you know it, the weather is better there than it is here."

I hang up, wallowing in the comfort of being understood at last. But as I start getting dressed for the final day of the short-game clinic, I realize I feel entirely different this morning. My body no longer aches. I feel well rested. And the sun is shining through the window.

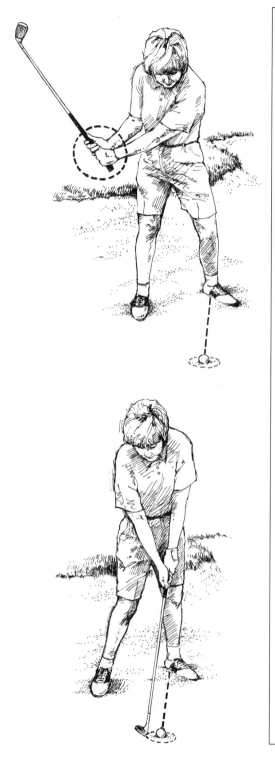

4. SAND PLAY

The rules of golf consider sand bunkers (also called sand traps) as hazards. This does not mean that you must take a penalty if you land in a sand bunker. What it does mean is that you may not take a practice swing inside the bunker or ground your club until you have started your downswing. If you do either of these things, you must take a two-stroke penalty.

You use a sand wedge for this shot because it has a lot of loft on it (about fifty-six degrees) and extra weight on the bottom of the clubhead that will help you lift the ball out of the bunker. If you don't have a sand wedge, use your pitching wedge. In either case, if you let your club do the work for you, you'll be surprised how easily you can make a recovery shot out of a bunker.

Sand Play Basics

A lot of people are afraid of sand shots. Don't be one of them! Just follow these guidelines:

The Set-Up:

1. You use an open stance, as you do for chipping and pitching, but your stance is wider. You want to settle your feet into the sand for stability.

2. Place your weight so that you favour your left (front) foot slightly.

Ball Position:

3. Position your feet so that the ball is towards your left (front) foot. Remember: left is for loft and you will need loft to get the ball over the lip of the bunker.

4. Imagine a circle in the sand surrounding the ball and aim your clubhead for the edge of the circle between you and the ball.

5. You will have to take some sand with your shot. In fact, it is the sand that will throw your ball out of the bunker. You hit the sand and then accelerate through the ball. To get height on the ball, a wristcock must be added.

Sandra's Tip: Many golfers are intimidated by bunkers, partly because they do not practise sand shots. Search out driving ranges and golf courses that provide practice sand bunkers. And practise!

My golf game responds in kind. Today, we practise sand play. Sand shots have an immediate visceral appeal for me. I *like* the idea of digging my feet into a bunker, as Sandra instructs us to do. It makes me feel grounded, secure. The swing Sandra shows us is short and its purpose is straightforward: all we want to do is get the ball up and out of the bunker. And to accomplish this, we must just let the fifty-plus-degree-angle of the sand wedge (or pitching wedge, if that's what you've chosen) do the work for us.

I make some terrible shots (of course), but this shot doesn't scare me. So what if I get sand in my face. I remember David's abject terror of sand bunkers and look forward to crowing about my sand-bunker-fear-free life. But I'll have to preface my crowing with an abject admission that he was right about today. Things *are* starting to click in again. And I can't put this dramatic change down to weather, because the air is still brisk. Much as I hate to admit it, David was right. Today compared to yesterday is day following night, light after darkness.

CHAPTER 6

BREAKTHROUGH

What a difference decent weather makes! It's the last week of May and it's finally warmed up. Nothing dramatic, mind you – I'm not wearing anything as radical as *shorts*. But today, for the first time, I'm not wearing a jacket or anything made of wool. My outfit: V-neck sweater, short-sleeved shirt, sleeveless undershirt, long pants . . . all of it cotton. I'm so accustomed to bundling up, I haven't realized how much freer it feels swinging a club without four layers of clothing in the way. The difference is as dramatic as skinny-dipping versus wearing a bathing suit.

And so to work. I'm back at the Golf Ranch. Sandra didn't expect me this morning. This is an intermediate group, she informs me crisply. Don't worry, I reply defensively, I'll just hang out and watch. Oh, okay, Sandra says, a bit reluctantly. Well, did I show her! But I'm getting ahead of my story.

First, the group is only *brushing* intermediate. Three of the women have taken Sandra's indoor winter clinic, so don't consider themselves beginners. The other two have played – but only a little. And it is definitely a WLM ensemble. Not only Women Like Me, but even a tiny bit *older*, on the whole. Our bones are well covered, as Sandra again wryly points out: "This group is well centred in our butts!" And it's a busty group (apart from me, a mere 34B). For the first time, the question of whether to make the classic V with your arms over or under the bust-line is debated. Just carry on through is Sandra's essential advice to the bustiest among us, a sizeable, white-haired woman of about sixty. She means *over* the bust. And if necessary, don't be afraid to lay on a little pressure. Don't let your bosom impede your progress!

My swing thought of the day is *follow through*. My backswing is okay – I've finally mastered the wristcock – but I don't finish. Which means, Sandra tells the assembled group, that I *decelerate* through the swing. In order to follow through correctly, in that lovely face-forward, chin-up, right-heel-off-the-ground position, you must *accelerate* through the swing. Keep moving! My problem, Sandra says, is the dreaded paralysis by analysis. I think too much about all the bits and pieces of the swing – stay balanced, keep the left arm straight, etc., etc. It's time to think of my golf swing as a single fluid motion. Rhythm is all.

Sandra demonstrates another common swing fault for our enlightenment, something she calls, appropriately, *casting* (as in casting for fish). When you "cast," you uncock your wrists too soon when you descend from the top of your backswing. You use too much arm motion and not enough body, and don't *feel* the weight of the club. The swing should be a pulling motion, not a pushing motion. Casting usually means you've gone back too far in your backswing. Sandra brilliantly demonstrates how a "casting" swing looks (and its unsatisfactory results), then immediately follows it with a good swing. Not for the first time, I'm amazed at how far and seemingly effortlessly her ball soars. I figure my best swing sends the ball approximately 20 per cent the distance of one of her throw-away swings. And Sandra might scoff at the hubris in even that figure.

Sandra re-emphasizes the crucial importance of the Four Basics. She runs through the three grips (Baseball, Overlapping, Interlocking) and inspects each of our grips. I try out all three and, to my surprise, the Overlapping Grip suddenly feels best: much more natural and comfortable than the Interlocking Grip, which now feels tight, unnatural, and constrictive. I test how hard I'm holding on and, lo and behold, I discover I'm holding the shaft lightly . . . like a baby bird! And this feels right. Sandra adjusts my grip to close a tiny gap that's opened up between my two hands and to move the second, third, and fourth fingers of my right hand forward slightly, so that they're visible on the front of the shaft.

"Don't think for a minute that this is something you learn and then have forever," Sandra says. "The pros constantly reinspect basics such as their grips – virtually every day." This surprises me, but I know it's true. I've started reading the golf section in the newspaper, and already I've read several stories about pros working on tiny swing faults. Tiger's coach drove from Houston to Irving, Texas, in the middle of the night during the Byron Nelson Classic a couple of weeks ago to help him fine-tune some minute problem he was having with his swing.

The pros also constantly take lessons, Sandra adds. "Contrast that with this statistic: Only one-third of golf-club members take lessons – and only 17 per cent of golfers overall! And the percentage would be even lower if we were talking only about men. Women take lessons much more often than men do. Ninety per cent of my beginners' clinics are women; I teach hundreds of you a season. Women want to do it right. Men are much more macho about the game: they just get out there and hack away."

It's four weeks now since *my* first lesson. I've hung out at a total of twelve group lessons. And what Sandra says about the importance of "Learning Golf Right" – that is, taking lessons from a pro – is beginning to be borne out . . . in me. Truth is, I'm feeling a tad cocky, because, in this group, Sandra considers me one of the best. This is certainly a first. She points out that we, as a group, do not find golf easy. In fact, her general rule about a natural golfer in every clinic is not true in this one. "You're all going to have to work at it," she tells us, contrasting us with some of her other clinics, which were filled with young, natural athletes. "But don't let this discourage you," she adds. "Remember, you don't have to be athletic to be a good golfer. But you do have to be disciplined. And a group of mature women like you should have no trouble with the discipline component of learning how to play a decent round of golf."

SANDRA'S SWING THOUGHT

GOLF IS A DISCIPLINED SPORT

Becoming a good golfer is much more about discipline than it is about being athletic. Add a little coordination and you're set.

Sandra has basically ignored me throughout this clinic and, unlike the last time this happened, I can handle it. Heck, I'm doing so well I don't need her attention! When she finally takes some notice, she's filled with accolades. "Hey! Look at you, Loral! I think it's time you got some clubs of your own." Until now, I've been using old clubs of David's, and Sandra has told me repeatedly that the shafts are far too stiff for me. She promises to advise me about how many clubs I need, and the right "flex" for the shafts.

I'm on top of the world as I drive home. Two weeks ago I turned fifty-three, and while I don't feel the slightest bit *old*, I have – until this moment, that is – more or less internalized the feeling that, at this stage of my life, I can't expect to master something completely new, complex, and different from the ground up. So today, the realization that I've actually learned a new skill from scratch comes as a rush. I can *do* it!!

My breakthrough coincides with a distressing break*down* by Tiger. Tiger, my shining light, what has happened to you? All the pundits were predicting he would win for the third time in a row and match Nick Price's 1973 record of three consecutive PGA-tournament wins. And what does he do? A wire-service story sums it up: "It was sudden, unexpected and a bit ugly . . . Tiger Woods saw his quest for a third-consecutive triumph almost disappear in a watery grave on No. 9 and brutally die with a double-bogey at 17." Ouch.

"What did I tell you?" David says. "I *told* you that Tiger was not about to win and win and win. Remember, golf is a game of nanomillimetres and the tiniest thing can interfere with your game."

"Well, not with mine!" I retort. "I'm enjoying the benefit of the finest instruction available and I'm progressing little by little – nanomillimetre by nanomillimetre if that's how you insist on describing it – and *my* progress is going in one direction and one direction only, straight ahead. In fact, today, I had a genuine breakthrough." I pause for effect.

David takes a long, hard look at me to see if I'm setting him up. Nope. He realizes I'm serious. He congratulates me, sincerely. Then he adds: "The secret is to build on it. Remember, you improve by tiny increments. And you *must* play regularly to add to those increments."

CHAPTER 7

CRASH AND BURN

On a Sunday afternoon at the Golf Ranch, I join a group of five high-school teachers who are taking their final lesson of a three-day long-game clinic. I've been fighting a nasty head cold since Friday, which makes me dopey, headachy, slightly dizzy. I head out to the Ranch against David's advice, confident that I can play through it.

It's a lovely summer's day, around 25°C, and this group of women is simply terrific. They're around my age, and they're bursting with humour, high spirits, and intelligence. They all know one another and have signed up for this clinic together. It's marvellous to watch them support and advise one another. And Sandra is really "on" today; she positively outdoes herself. The women are all at different levels, so she individualizes her teaching to relate to each one of them separately. I'm amazed, as always, at the ease with which she remembers names.

My swing thought for the day is: Stop breaking the swing down into its component parts. *Just relax and let it happen.*

I start by hitting a couple of decent balls. No one sees them, of course. Then disaster strikes. Sandra is telling us that golf is a game of adjustments and that we must get used to changing clubs and, with each change, change our set-up accordingly. She instructs us to count out twenty-five balls and hit two or three balls with each club.

I'm not listening closely and I don't get it straight that I'm to change clubs every few balls. I just keep hitting blindly, blankly, with my 9-iron (which I still can't tell from a 6-iron: I can never remember which way you're supposed to read the number on the sole of the club). I silently repeat my swing thought, *Relax and let it happen.* I'm in a kind of trance when Sandra notices I'm not doing what she has instructed. She comes along and hands me a giant driver. "Here. Try this, Loral. Now remember, grip down on the shaft," she instructs. I do, but it doesn't work. I've never even picked up a driver before (the only wood I've hit with is a 5-wood), let alone tried to hit anything with one. The giant clubhead on this driver looks like a shillelagh, like something the Flintstones might have used to hunt possum with. I hit the ground several times in a row with the clubhead, removing a square foot or so of turf.

Then I do something I've never, ever done: I hit the ball straight up in the air, at a ninety-degree angle. Then I hit it sharply to the right. Then I dribble it along the ground. Then I whiff . . . and whiff . . . and whiff. Clearly, I'm bent on performing every indecent act ever committed on a golf ball.

Guardian angel of new golfers, where are you when I need you? I'm burning with embarrassment. I keep hanging on to my swing thought like a condemned person clings to a prayer: *Relax and let it happen.* And then I notice that Sandra is taking an inordinate interest in me. She stands directly behind me. I can't see her, but I *know* she's there. And I get worse. And worse. And then Sandra, with maddening ebullience, asks the group to help me: "Loral's having a really hard time today. What can you suggest to her?"

Whereupon the entire group stops what they're doing and turns their collective gaze upon me. They outdo themselves with solicitous suggestions. They're *teachers,* for heaven's sake. They're in the business of guidance, advice, encouragement,

---

SANDRA'S TEACHING TIP

TAKE ONLY ONE SWING THOUGHT WITH YOU

We call thinking too much *paralysis by analysis*. If you think too much, your golf swing is not going to happen instinctively.

When you go to play a round of golf, take only one swing thought with you, such as "finish in balance." And when you get to the golf course, don't try to remember everything you've been working on on the practice tee. Just tell yourself to relax and let your golf swing happen.

---

possessed of unbearable niceness of being. One by one, they give me counsel, in the most congenial, empathetic way. Their words swirl around me in a blur. And then, through the fog, I hear Sandra's spritely voice: "What are *you* thinking, Loral?"

I answer: "Funny thing, every time I hit the ball I keep thinking to myself that the *next* one is going to be great." Whereupon I hit the ball with my massive driver, gouge the ground in front of the ball, and remove about half a block of earth.

What must Sandra be thinking? I feel embarrassed for *her*. After all these lessons, by one of the best golfers Canada has ever known, now regarded as one of the best golf teachers there is . . . I mean, is there any hope for me – this woman who admits to not being athletic, who tries so hard but . . . ?

I feel dizzy. If I don't drink some water, I'm going to faint. I bolt for the bathroom. Sandra will assume I'm cracking under pressure, I think dully as I flee. But if I tell her I'm feeling sick, she'll think I'm a hypochondriac! There's no way out. I've watched *her* for more than five weeks now, and she works round the clock, six and seven days a week, never complaining, never crying sick or exhausted.

I drive home in a daze, stopping at a drugstore to load up on Aspirin, cold remedies, antihistamines. I get home, swallow some pills, take the phone off the hook, and go to bed. Mercifully, I fall into a dead sleep.

I awake around 8 P.M., feeling groggy, headachy, unable to cope with life. I reconnect the phone. Within seconds, it rings. It's David, just checked into

The Briars golf resort at Jackson's Point on Lake Simcoe, in anticipation of Peter Gzowski's annual golf tournament for literacy. I grind out my tale of woe. He listens sympathetically. Until this moment, the stories about being humiliated by golf, which I've read *ad nauseam* and which people like Ken Rodmell have told me, have been purely academic exercises: I understand intellectually what they're saying, but can't imagine ever taking a game seriously enough for this to happen to me. And now it's happened. I am in a state of supreme agony over what those teachers must have thought. I am in a state of supreme agony about embarrassing Sandra. I am convinced that Sandra is dreading the rest of the summer with this clinging, hopeless, wannabe golfer hanging around while she's just trying to do her job – send every one of her students home with an improved golf swing and golf game. Should I tell Sandra I was sick today and *that* was why I did so badly? But if I tell her this, she'll probably think I can't take the pressure!

I pour all this out to David, who listens intently and then delivers his advice: "You've *got* to start practising, every day. You can't leave it all to Sandra and the Golf Ranch. You can practise in the backyard. You just put something down on the ground in front of you – it can be the *Toronto Star*, for heaven's sake – and practise your swing over and over and over again. That's how you groove your swing, get it into your muscle memory. You swing over and over again. A few hundred times, for starters."

Groove your swing. This is one of David's pet phrases, I remember. One of the many, about golf, that have been sublimely meaningless until now. *Groove your swing.* I repeat the phrase in my fogged brain. Could I really do that? The awful, shameful truth is I have not *once* practised my swing at home. And I've only been to a driving range once, with David. Meanwhile, I've listened over and over again to Sandra's advice about the necessity to practise, practise. And I've done nothing.

It's time to start. No matter that I live in a narrow city house visible to neighbours from every angle. If I practise on the front deck, my ever-friendly neighbour Sam across the street will be sure to make comments; if I practise in the back garden, I'll be subjected to the scrutiny of Domenic, who spends long hours all summer tending his sumptuous vegetable garden.

Well, I have no choice. These things I will simply have to endure. In the name of golf.

CHAPTER 8

PAINFUL RECOVERY

I am joining David late today at Jackson's Point, *not* to participate in the Peter Gzowski golf tournament but to attend the annual Red Barn theatre performance the night before. Every year, Peter hosts an old-fashioned variety-show-cum-revue in the Red Barn, a drafty wooden barn that functions as a summer theatre. And every year the line-up of Canadian talent, both new and seasoned, is unpredictable and thrilling. I wouldn't miss it for the world.

As for the golf: it starts at eight the following morning, preceded by a buffet breakfast and bagpipes. We always rent a cottage across the street with a group of friends and, as the strains of the bagpipes waft over Lake Simcoe, I drive off, back to work in the city. The golfers include many of the performers from the night before, plus numerous media and corporate heavyweights. At a luncheon following the tournament, a designated "poet laureate" reads a poem specially composed for the day, much schmoozing occurs, and a grand time is had by all.

As for me: I get my annual patriotic high at the Red Barn and then beat a hasty retreat. The rest of it intimidates the hell out of me. In twelve years, I have not once ventured across the street to join the golfers' breakfast or even look at the tee-off area. This year, knowing I would be immersed in golf by the time it rolled around, I wondered if things would be different. Would I perhaps feel at home among these golfers and celebrities for the first time?

No, I would not. Nothing has changed. It's the day after my debacle with the teachers at the Golf Ranch and not only am I feeling a complete failure at golf, I'm feeling like a complete golf fraud.

I arrive to find David enjoying a golf post-mortem with the foursome he has just finished playing with in a warm-up round before tomorrow's tournament. They're sitting out on the patio behind the cottage overlooking Lake Simcoe, drinking gin and tonics and passing around salsa and tortilla chips. The foursome consists of David, Ken Rodmell, Martin O'Malley, one of David's long-standing golf cronies, and Jack Rabinovitch, a newcomer to the group. I join them for a drink and proceed to whine about my humiliation with Sandra and the teachers yesterday. As always, Ken is a true mensch. He's told me in the past that *nothing* in his life has humiliated him to the extent that golf has. When I tell him I have humiliated not only myself but Sandra, he is all empathy. "Don't worry, Loral," he says soothingly. "I've had lessons from George Knudson and I still can't play golf worth a damn."

Jack Rabinovitch is a compact package of a man, somewhere in his sixties. I know and admire him by reputation as a patron of all the right causes as well as the founder of the Giller literary prize, which he established in honour of his late wife. But I've never met him before in a small social group. He proves to be a congenial fellow, but here's the rub: During a visit to Florida *two months ago*, Jack decided to take up golf. So . . . he took a few lessons, first from one pro and then from another, more helpful, one. And now he's playing with David, Martin, and Ken as if it were the most natural, normal thing in the world. And they're saying things like "He has a very nice swing" and "He's doing very well." *And* he's playing in the tournament tomorrow. I simply cannot stand it. Jack has to be at least ten years older than I am, and he probably weighs no more than I do. So nobody can attribute his instant golf success to youthful brawn.

Damn.

I kiss David goodbye the next morning as he heads across the street to breakfast and the tournament. "Enjoy!" I shout, as I climb into the car to head back to Toronto. A few miles south, I stop at a public driving range beside the road. Time to follow through and *practise*. I pull into a small parking area in front of a squalid, flat-roofed cement-block building. As I get out of the car and look at it, I understand what the movie *Tin Cup* was driving at with its depiction of Kevin Costner as lord of all he surveys at an end-of-the-road driving range. This place is truly grungy. A dishevelled fellow with a grey stubble of beard and black encrusted fingernails is standing behind a window counter. Behind him yawns a dark interior cavity in which I can dimly see a couple of shelves filled with metal buckets of balls. A small, rusty bucketful of filthy, unmatched balls costs five dollars. "There's about forty balls in there," Grey Stubble says, leaning across the counter with a leer and digging his fingernails into a bucket to show me what a bargain I'm getting.

"I'll take it," I say, handing him a five-dollar bill. A young woman with a baby in a stroller beside her is receiving instruction at the nearest tee from a young man. Otherwise, the range is empty. I head for the farthest tee, where I can be alone and where there's a smidgen of shade. It's a muggy day, with a threat of thunderstorm in the air. The tees are rubber; they poke up from dirty rubber mats speckled with bald spots that presumably once were treads.

This is a new golf experience. To think I labelled the Golf Ranch basic! My shoes are killing me. I take them off and practise in my sock feet on my mat. The right corner of the mat curls gently upward, the grass ahead is brown and broken, but I no longer care about the aesthetics of this place. The feel of the mat under my sock feet is strangely freeing. In fact, I feel good, standing here in my socks, cars whizzing by on the highway a few feet behind me, swinging away with absolutely *no one* to watch or critique. I empty my rusty bucket in twenty minutes, getting away a total of three really good balls. They travel about eighty yards, dead straight, and the *sound* is right. The golf virus will truly infect you when you hit three good shots in a row, David says. Mine aren't in a row.

Our car is not air-conditioned, and the temperature and humidity are rising precipitously as I drive home. I'm going to have to plan my practice sessions early or late in the day. I watch for driving ranges closer to home as I drive south. The closest I find I clock at forty minutes one way, in non-rush-hour traffic. If I practise in the morning, I'll go after the morning rush hour – but not too long after or I'll run into midday heat. Afternoons for the next month or so are going to be brutally hot, so the other practice alternative is early evening, after the afternoon rush hour. Golf is tricky and time-consuming for a city dweller. I remember why I've never had time for it before.

I survey our back garden when I get home. It's about fifteen yards from our deck to the garage. And five-foot fences, about six yards apart, flank both sides. Not quite the challenge an inner-city tenement dweller faces when looking for a place to groove her swing, maybe, but more than the average suburbanite has to cope with! We have a big pine tree; perhaps I'll practise by hitting pine cones. Dianne planted this idea during our North Carolina visit: the pine cones on the golf course there were immense, perfect for practice shots. I haul a winter doormat out of the basement and place it at the bottom of our deck. Just the right size for a teeing mat. I gather a basket of pine cones. I lay my pitching wedge, 9-, 7-, and 5-irons against the steps of the deck. I stretch out my back, vigorously swinging two clubs at a time, then follow with the golf-club-across-the-shoulder stretch that I find so hard to coordinate. All set.

I remember Sandra's practice instructions: *Start with the short irons and work your way up.* I start with my pitching wedge. The mat works fine. The pine cones aren't great (these are shaped like cigars, not as easy to hit as the fat, upright North Carolina variety), but they help me focus on the "ball" and keep my head down. I hit most of the pine cones as far as a planter midway between my "golf station" and garage; a few travel as far as the garage. I'm enjoying this, just like I enjoyed the grungy practice range up the highway. No one to correct me! Just whack away "grooving my swing." Domenic is shuffling quietly on the other side of the fence, examining his tomato plants. He pretends to take no notice. Good. I think this is going to work.

The next day I drive to the range that I clocked forty minutes away. I run into a bit more traffic than I'd expected, plus some construction, but I make it in less than an hour. This range is much more up-market: there's a proper walk-in trailer with two summer students running it, and even some golf equipment for sale in a little shop inside. The driving range is four times the size of the grunge range, and they're "all grass tees," as the highway billboard promises. About half the tees are filled; a few dozen men and two women hitting mighty balls with drivers. Welcome to the world of golf.

I choose a tee at the far end of the line, with my back to everyone else. I like the feeling of practising alone. "There's no point in going out to a driving range and blindly hitting fifty balls," I remember Sandra telling us during her class on alignment. "Golf is a target game. When you practise, always take the time to align your balls with a target." I carefully align my balls with a 100-yard flag. My results are okay. Nothing spectacular, but nothing like my infamous high-school-teacher debacle. I hit the balls fairly consistently about a hundred yards, maybe half of them in the air, 60 to 70 per cent of them straight.

I feel as if I'm getting into a physical rhythm at last. It feels good. I resolve to groove my swing every day, even if it's only fifteen minutes in the back garden, alone with my pine cones. Consistency. Rhythm. Regularity. *Remember, you improve by tiny increments. And you must practise regularly to add to these increments.*

CHAPTER 9

LORAL HITS IT THICK
ON A "PAR-9" HOLE

The U.S. Open is upon us and Andy and Dianne have invited us to watch it Sunday at their place. I'm all for it. It's exactly two months since the Masters, and I've come a long way. I not only read the newspaper golf pages now, I understand at least half of what I read without thumbing through the glossary in one of my golf manuals or asking David for guidance. And besides, I love hanging out with Andy and Dianne.

As David goes out the door for an appointment early Thursday morning, he calls, "Three to 7:30." Huh? I ask. "The Open," he replies. "Starts at 3 this afternoon, goes on until 7:30." Oh. My heart thuds. Yes, of course. How could I forget that these tournaments take *four days?*

I tune in and out on Thursday, Friday, and Saturday. But Sunday, David wants to be at Andy and Dianne's the moment TV coverage begins, and I know it won't be over for at least four hours. I can't take refuge in charisma today: Tiger Woods and another Mr. Charisma, Australia's Greg Norman, are out of the running, and the leaders are less than mesmerizing – Ernie Els, a boring South African, Colin Montgomerie, a moody Scot who feels hard done by because he's just missed winning several majors, and Tom Lehman, a nondescript American. "I figure I'm at the bread-and-circuses stage of my golf education," I confide to Dianne. "I find I need glamour, pizzazz, youth, charisma, to keep me focused over four hours."

"That's absolutely normal," Dianne says. Once again, I thank the golf gods for Dianne.

Lehman hits the ball off the tee and takes a huge divot. "I guess he hit *that* one awfully thick," I say, hoping everyone will realize how quietly knowledgeable I have become. A loud collective guffaw rebounds around the room.

"You mean fat," Andy says, as the laughter subsides.

"You hit the ball thin . . . you hit the ball thick . . ." I say, my voice trailing off.

"No," Andy replies in a kindly tone. "You hit the ball thin – or you hit it fat. You can't hit it thick."

Oh.

I shut up for a time. Then somebody hits the ball "pin high." "What in God's name does that mean?" I ask. Dianne doesn't know either. We turn to Andy and David for guidance. First one, then the other, tries to explain. Dianne and I look at them blankly. They become exasperated and shush us while they watch the next shot. "I really want to know," I whine.

"Yes, we really want to know," Dianne bleats. A commercial break gives Andy an excuse to capitulate.

"Okay, girls," he says, "this is what it means." He pushes three plates on the coffee table into a row. "Pin high means hitting the ball parallel with the pin [flagstick], at right angles from where you shoot the ball."

"Oh," I reply. What sublimely daft terminology! I remember Sandra's quip at my first golf clinic: "Yes, I'm bilingual: I speak English and I speak golf."

The tournament continues, the golfspeak waxes thick (fat?). As the exciting finish approaches, someone hits a soft draw. *Hunh?* "Oh, that means hitting the ball slightly to the left," David explains.

"If it were more extreme, it would be a hard hook," Andy adds helpfully.

Andy makes his living by drawing political cartoons. David radiates humour. And neither of them sees any humour in the distinction between a soft draw and a hard hook. I thought I'd come a long way in this golf thing. Clearly, I haven't.

Friends of Andy and Dianne's arrive around five o'clock. They've just finished a round of golf. "We're spending 'quality time' together," Tom says drily, as they come in.

"I never thought I'd be watching golf on TV!" Sandy sighs, as she sprawls on the rug in front of the television set.

I've met Sandy once before with Dianne and felt an instant rapport. She's just turned fifty, she and Tom have been married fourteen years; it's a

second marriage for both of them and they share three children from their first marriages. She's a real-estate agent; he's an executive in a public-relations firm – both demanding jobs with unpredictable hours. Tom loves golf passionately; Sandy never thought she had time or interest in taking it up. But Tom, a driven, hardworking man who exudes intensity, is clearly the kind of guy who has to be *doing* something. And the only place he can unwind is on the golf course. Between the demands of his job and his need to unwind – on the golf course – there's precious little time for him and Sandy. Solution? Sandy takes up golf, which provides a framework for spending time together.

This vehicle of togetherness seems to be working. "We spent a nice 'down' time together playing golf today, just the two of us," Sandy says. "I've been playing for two years now and, yes, I'm enjoying it," she continues. "But I don't *love* it. Not yet, anyway. Nine holes is enough for me. And even if I wanted to, I don't have *time* for eighteen holes."

It's an exciting finish as golf finishes go: an unprecedented four front-runners, one to two strokes apart. In the end, Ernie Els, the South African, wins. I try to rise above externals and appreciate his inner golf greatness.

The Open over at last, we retire downstairs to dinner. The conversation is monochromatic: golf, golf, more golf. "God, I remember how boring some evenings were before I took up golf," Sandy says. She pulls a face: "Now, let me tell you about that *incredible* 'par-9' hole I played last week . . ." I'd tuned out for a moment, but the animation in Sandy's voice brings me back.

"Oh, *tell* us about it!" I trill. "Were you playing really well that day?"

CHAPTER 10

FIRST ROUND

It's been six weeks. I've attended four of Sandra's full-swing clinics and three of her short-game clinics – not every lesson in every clinic, but the total is adding up. I've been present at eighteen group lessons in all. And I've been practising, at three different driving ranges and in my little backyard sanctuary, my "golf station," as I affectionately call it. I've been to school, and I've done my homework. Time to move into a bigger world.

"I sense it's time to light out for the territories," I say to Sandra, as she and John pack up after the third lesson of another short-game clinic at Oakville Executive.

"*Yes!*" Sandra replies, her face lighting up. I accept her enthusiasm in the spirit in which I know it is intended. We both know we're weary of each other's company. For now. Enough, already. Time to move on.

Sharon has been calling me for several weeks now, inviting me out to play. She's clearly bemused by all these lessons plus practise, practise, practise. "When are you going to throw caution to the winds and actually go *golfing*, Loral?" she asks delicately.

"Well," I say, "now, at last, I'm ready." Good. Sharon knows just the course to get started on. It's called Flemingdon Park, a semi-public course, and we can get there in thirty minutes without going near an expressway. Perfection.

I tell David. "What's your tee time?" he says.

"We can't book one by phone," I reply. "I'm just picking Sharon up tomorrow morning at nine."

"You *must* be joking!" David contorts his face into an expression of arrant horror. "Tomorrow's *Friday*. You're mad to go near a public golf course in the city on a Friday morning on a beautiful day in June. As I speak, people all over Toronto are calling in sick at the office so that they can go golfing. Trust me, it's going to be crowded, *really* crowded. And you're going to be slow. You're going to hold people up and there is *nothing* more irritating than being held up. Be sensible: wait until Monday morning."

I'm deflated. It's taken me six weeks to gear myself up to *a real golf course* . . . and now this. I call Sharon. As ever, Sharon is pragmatic. "Look, we can wait until Monday. It's only three more days."

On Monday morning, Sharon guides me through familiar residential neighbourhoods a few kilometres northeast of our house, then a small business section, past some highrises, and down a steep hill into a leafy ravine. And suddenly we're there – in a beautiful park in a deep valley that feels miles from the city.

We park under the shade of two big trees and head across a gravel parking area towards the clubhouse. The clubhouse looks like a summer cottage from the 1950s. It's small and made of wood; it has a long, low, sloping roof and freshly painted rust-red walls with windows trimmed in white. We cross a stone patio with small white tables shaded by generous trees, and open a screen door into a coffee shop with fake-wood walls, small metal tables and chairs, and a menu

---

SANDRA'S TIP

GOLF COURSE PROTOCOL

Every golf course makes its own rules about tee-off times (sometimes you can book a time by phoning ahead; sometimes you simply have to wait your turn). Greens fees vary widely; usually (not always), pullcarts or electric carts cost extra. Some courses require you to rent a golf cart (to speed up play); some, like Flemingdon, do not have electric carts. Many courses have reduced junior, senior, twilight, or weekday rates. Some, like Flemingdon, have free practice facilities; others have full-sized driving ranges where you "buy" buckets of practice balls. The bottom line: It's always best to call the pro shop first and find how the course operates.

---

behind a counter offering hotdogs, hamburgers, sandwiches, cookies, and soft drinks. About a dozen people are sitting drinking coffee or lining up for tee-off times – young men, young women, couples, middle-aged women. They're dressed in everything from Bermuda shorts, shirts with collars, visors – the standard golf gear Sandra has instructed me to wear – to jeans and sneakers. Nobody is grungy, nobody is dressed to the nines. The common denominator: tidiness and comfort.

The first available tee-off time is 11:40 A.M., the young man in charge tells us. Well, it's only 10 A.M., but we're not going home now. No alternative but to "button down" the hatches. It's a nine-hole course and costs $17, $5 more for a pullcart. I've brought only four clubs – a 7-iron, a 9-iron, a pitching wedge, and a putter – so I'll carry my bag.

We head over to the practice area, which is free of charge. I've never seen anything like *this* before. It consists of a huge, billowing net, like a circus safety-net, except it's anchored to the ground inside a metal frame about twenty feet high. In front of it are scuffed, muddy mats with rubber tees. Bring your own balls. Sharon and I hunker down and hit balls into the net. Good practice, I suppose, although we never quite know if we've hit the ball well or not because it can't travel any distance.

Brooks/Kalinsky on the tee, Dean/Kawaguchi in the hole. "That's us," Sharon says. "It means we're up after Brooks and Kalinsky tee off." We walk over to a small area between the practice net and the coffee-shop patio where people are lacing up golf shoes, cleaning golf clubs, sorting through golf bags and putting them on carts.

"Why didn't the loudspeaker say Dean/Thomas?" I ask.

"They know we're playing together, so they just announce one of our names," Sharon explains. "The other name means we're being paired up with somebody else. It's usually two other people."

As we approach the waiting area, a tall, dark-haired young man extends his hand. "Hi. I'm Ron and this is my wife, Dana. I think we're going to be playing with you." Dana and Ron are Japanese-Canadian, both about thirty. Dana, tiny and trim, is wearing a stylish round-brimmed straw hat, trendy oval sunglasses, enormous gold earrings, and bright-pink lipstick that perfectly matches her pink T-shirt and shorts. She confides shyly that she's only been playing for three months: "But Ron's been playing *much* longer!"

"On the tee: Dean/Kawaguchi." Ron tees off first from the men's tee, which is behind us. He hits the ball beautifully, about 150 yards. Sharon, Dana, and I head over to the women's tee, directly in front of the coffee-shop patio. This is the moment I'm supposed to be so nervous about. But no one is sitting on the patio, so I only have Sharon and Dana to worry about. "You go first," we say to Dana. Dana stands up between the tee markers as tall as she can manage, grasping a huge driver. She takes a couple of slow, tentative-looking practice swings. Then she goes for it. Her ball skids along the ground about twenty yards. Well, *that* certainly takes some pressure off. Sharon goes next, using her 3-wood, and hits the ball a presentable eighty yards or so, slightly leftward.

My turn. I look down the fairway, a beautiful expanse of grass, the putting green shimmering atop a hillock in the distance (it's 245 yards away according to the scorecard we were given when we paid our greens fee). I'm using my 7-iron. I take a couple of practice swings, being careful to brush the grass as Sandra has instructed. Then I let it fly. To my joy, I hit the ball dead straight, about the same distance as Sharon. Whew. Hurdle number one surmounted.

We're off. I hitch my bag over my shoulder and stride down the fairway towards

SANDRA'S TEACHING TIP

THE PRE-SHOT ROUTINE

Golf is a very disciplined sport, and all good golfers have a pre-shot routine that they follow every time they hit the ball. Since every shot is different, you need something constant to help you set your tempo and keep your focus every time you hit the ball.

Your pre-shot routine should go something like this:

1. Stand behind the golf ball and visualize your target.

2. As you walk towards the shot, take a couple of practice swings to help you stretch out your back muscles (they may have tightened up since your last shot) and also to help you set your tempo.

3. Now put your clubhead down on target and commit your feet.

4. Take your grip.

When you're a new golfer, all this may sound very complex. Eventually, the more you play, it will all come naturally before you make a shot.

my ball. I've gone about ten yards when I realize I've forgotten Dana. Oh yes, she has to hit next, and her ball is only a few steps away. Sharon and I hang back, trying to be unobtrusive, while we wait for Dana to hit the ball. Ron walks ahead with Dana, talking quietly to her. Dana gets to her ball, sets her cart down, fiddles with her sunglasses and hat. Then she sorts through her golf bag, which is large and stuffed with clubs. Eventually, she pulls out an iron and takes three slow, deliberate practice swings. Then she hits the ball another twenty yards.

Now I know what David meant. I bite my lip, try to "rise above," as David counsels in trying moments. I use my 7-iron again for my second shot off the fairway. It travels another eighty yards or so, well up in the air and straight. I can barely contain my excitement; I want to race after my ball. But it's Sharon's turn, and she tops her ball; it skitters along the ground. This means my ball is ahead of hers. And, of course, Dana's is behind both of ours. *Calma, calma,* I tell myself. *Rise above*. Take a leaf out of Ron's book: his ball is away ahead of all of ours, but is he in a hurry? No, he's sticking close to Dana, quietly helping her with every shot.

We take two and three-quarter hours to play nine holes. Yes, this falls far short of Sandra's "ready golf" ideal, but I take no responsibility for our collective slowness! And I understand perfectly now why Dianne couldn't be bothered with putting for the first two years or so that she played. I rush through putting, paying no attention at all to what I'm doing. What seems vitally important is making it from tee-off to green as fast as possible, and in as few shots as possible. Hitting those long shots seems *terribly* important.

And I love Flemingdon. It feels like a nineteenth-century English landscape painting, with luxuriant weeping willows all round, woodlands, hills, and dales, and a picturesque river (the Don) running through. Today is cool and moist, with a scent of rain in the air, and we seem to float inside a misty light. No matter that a couple of holes are overlooked by highrises, and there's a faint city rumble in the distance. *In toto*, it feels completely pastoral.

I am ecstatic about my game. What I find most gratifying are my fairway shots: I consistently hit clean and straight, an average of eighty yards. Being teamed up with Dana makes me feel like Sandra Post in comparison! Ron is astoundingly patient with her, always encouraging, occasionally counselling, never rushing her. Dana bends both arms completely double when she swings, in both directions – backswing and follow-through. Her swing is a perfect object lesson in how *not* to

---

SANDRA'S TEACHING TIP

THE BASICS OF SCORING

A full round of golf includes eighteen holes. Each hole has a "par," which means the optimum number of strokes required to get the ball from tee-off into the hole. Holes are designated par 3, par 4, or par 5, depending on the distance from tee to hole. Average par over eighteen holes is 72. If you score one stroke above par (for example, six strokes on a par-5 hole), you *bogey* the hole. If you score one stroke under par (four strokes on a par-5 hole), you *birdie* the hole. That's all you need to know to get started!

do it. Oh, I feel so smug and superior. "Now, no more chicken wings!" Ron says gently, as Dana prepares to tee off. After all I've heard about impatient husbands on golf courses, Ron surely is a marvel.

I hit almost all of my fairway shots with my trusty 7-iron. I don't see why, really, I should ever graduate to a driver or, indeed, a wood of any kind. And speaking of clubs: As David told me would happen, all of a sudden the various clubs seem very easy to differentiate. All that agonizing over which clubs are the short ones and which are the long, and how the numbers they carry stupidly run opposite to their lengths, and my confusion between the purpose of woods and the purpose of irons, and all that stuff about loft that seemed silly and superfluous . . . funny, it all seems straightforward now.

As for my score: Well, I hit the ball eighty-four times! On a 35-par round (half-round?). Fifty shots on the fairway and thirty-four strokes on the putting green. Sharon shot 64, or so she claims. I tend to disbelieve her ever so slightly. She took lots of "mulligans" off the tee, and most of the time she didn't hit the ball very far. She also hit into the water and the woods several times (*I* didn't hit the ball out of bounds even once). And did she take penalties for those shots? I don't think so!

CHAPTER 11

GOLF HONEYMOON

David and I are driving north to Parry Sound, where we share a cottage property with my parents, who live there half the year. We'll be there for four days, a perfect opportunity to play the Parry Sound Golf & Country Club with David. He's played it several times, and pronounces it a hardy Canadian Shield–based course that is "very hard on the legs." Hmmph! I was born in Parry Sound, and pre-Cambrian rock is part of my heritage. I've tromped over it many times in search of the perfect basket of wild blueberries and playing golf on it sounds pretty tame to me.

I've booked a tee-off time at 1:50 P.M. As we drive north it rains steadily. The sky erupts with the heaviest downpour yet, just as we're approaching Parry Sound. We must telephone the golf course and cancel immediately, David says firmly. It's 12:40 P.M., seventy minutes before tee-off time. "Let's wait and see what happens,"

I suggest, adding, "Sandra says, 'If you're going to be a golfer, you have to be an optimist.'" We stop at a grocery store to stock up for the weekend. Thirty minutes later, when we emerge, the sky has cleared. "Oh, look! The rain has stopped," I say.

David looks sceptical: "Why don't we cancel? We'll play tomorrow."

"They're predicting unsettled weather all weekend," I say stubbornly. "It's not raining now, we've got a tee-off time booked, we're not expected by Mom and Dad until after five. Why don't we go for it?"

Truth is, I'm *psyched*, as our kids would say. It's been four days since my marvellous Flemingdon round, and I feel a need to get out in the open, to stretch my muscles. In fact, I can hardly wait to get out there; I'm really excited about playing. And there's something else: A thousand tasks and responsibilities await me at the cottage. Is golf entering a new space in my head – a space that spells release, escape?

I called Sandra after my round with Sharon at Flemingdon to tell her how great everything was. I told her I plan next to play with David. "You play your game and let him play his," she counselled. "And don't feel you have to listen to what he tells you to do." I promised to follow her advice.

The rain holds off and David relents. He's very tough with me on the first two holes, telling me where to lay down my clubs, how not to enter a sand bunker (from the far end), to hurry up and putt (just as I'm lining up the ball and trying to steady my nerves). But by the third hole, he backs off. We're *not* holding up the people behind us and he realizes I *have* learned a few things from all those clinics with Sandra.

I love every minute, indeed every second, of this nine-hole round. To think I thought I loved Flemingdon! It has *nothing* on the Parry Sound course. I've spent about thirty summers in the Parry Sound area and I love its topography as I love my children. It feels like home. And this golf course brings me back in the most visceral way: the smells, the vegetation, the small animals and birds – even the mosquitoes are old, dear friends.

I am so blindly lovestruck with it all that when one of my balls ends up between two huge outcroppings of pre-Cambrian granite – literally between a rock and hard place and impossible to hit without destroying either the club or my arm – I burble on about the transformative metaphors inherent in this impossible lie.

SANDRA'S TIPS

UNPLAYABLE LIES

If you have hit a ball against a rock, a tree, or some other immovable object, don't take a chance of hurting yourself and causing permanent injury. Take a penalty, and you'll be a lot healthier for it. Measure two club lengths away from the obstruction (parallel or behind it, never closer to the hole). Then drop the ball and play the shot, or play a ball as close as possible to the spot from which the original ball was last played. You incur a one-stroke penalty.

David does not share these passions. For starters, he *hates* the weather. It's a muggy day, but (my view) not unbearable. And he abominates mosquitoes. But the real bottom line is that his golf is "intermittent" (his word) today. The five or six soaring shots he hits go either into the woods (and he loses them completely) or into the rough. Over our nine holes, he loses four balls. "Well, that's *one* thing you don't have to worry about with me," I say sunnily, in a tone that I know is infuriatingly smug. "I may not hit the ball far, but at least I always know where it is." This does not seem to make him happier.

David hits one drive with his new Bubble Burner driver the farthest (he says) that he's ever hit a drive – about three hundred yards. I'm not entirely sure how he knows how far he has hit it, because this is one of the balls he loses. And this is as much my fault as it is his, he tells me, because I didn't stand behind him and watch where the ball was going, the way a golfing partner is supposed to do. I also commit the unpardonable sin of talking while his ball is in the air, rabbiting on about what a good shot it is. He cuts me off sharply, informing me that one has to be quiet as well as vigilant after hitting a drive, so that you can *hear* as well as see (or hear instead of see?) where the ball goes. Oh dear. I'm plainly a failure at all this golf etiquette and protocol.

Over gin and tonics in our cottage kitchen, David becomes generous. "You're addressing the ball well," he says. "You're hitting the ball a fair distance, and you're getting it into the air pretty consistently. And that shot you hit out of the

> ## SANDRA'S TIP
>
> ### LEARN THE RULES OF GOLF ONE AT A TIME
>
> The rules of golf originated in Scotland at the Royal and Ancient Golf Association and they've been adapted in Canada by the Royal Canadian Golf Association (RCGA). You can buy the book of rules for a nominal fee at the RCGA or at your golf club. In the United States, rule books are available from the United States Golf Association (USGA) in Far Hills, New Jersey. The rules of golf can be very complex, but nobody expects you to learn them all at once or, indeed, to sit down and read them through. The best way to learn the rules is through experience as you come across them, one at a time.
>
> That said, rules are a very important part of golf. It's the only game I know where a competitor will actually call a rule on himself, even if no one else witnessed it. Golf is a game of honour and you are responsible for your own infractions in the game.
>
> Knowing the rules of golf enhances your enjoyment and appreciation of the game. And if you want to play in any tournament, you must know the rules.

bunker was brilliant. *I would have been there for weeks.*" Well, thank you, Sandra. You've taught me all I know about sand bunkers, including, probably, the most important lesson of all: not to be afraid of them. When the subject of my putting comes up, David praises one five-footer I holed, "the very length that confounds the pros when their nerves go. But," he continues, "I'm afraid your putting in general is irredeemably ugly." Ouch. He doesn't approve of my cross-handed grip, and he says I have no sense of tempo.

But he says I'm hitting the ball about 120 yards fairly often. Gosh. I didn't realize it was going that far. If I'm hitting it 120 yards without fully following through (which I'm not), and with a short backswing and a mere 7-iron . . . the mind reels at my potential. Maybe 200 yards once I get going? Feeling that promise of power through my shoulders, back, arms, and body is exhilarating. As Sandra says, women aren't used to swinging freely through their shoulders and, now that I'm doing it, I love the sense of release. I know I will improve. Training and practice will build my swing. Why not? Right now, I'm hitting at *least* three out of five of my tee and fairway shots straight down the middle of the fairway. I feel no sense of restriction because of my age.

"But the big question is, do you have the click?" David asks later in the evening.

"Yes, yes!" I cry. And I do, I really do. I can't wait to get out again. "Let's get up early tomorrow morning and have a round," I say. David demurs. Now why would he be reluctant? As for me, I not only feel the "click," I feel the beginnings of an obsession coming over me. Golf is marvellously freeing. It's a wonderful escape from the demands of real life. And here, at Deep Bay, I don't even have to gear myself up for a long drive to and from the course.

Thirty hours later, at 5 A.M. on the longest day of the year, I crawl out of bed, in the dark, leaving David sound asleep. I feel like a six-year-old running away from home. If I can just get past the corner store where they know me, I'll have a clean getaway. I tiptoe past my parents' cottage and I'm off – down Highway 69, which is eerily empty for the first time in memory. I put my foot on the gas pedal and accelerate into the early-morning light.

It's a classic first day of summer in Northern Ontario. Clear sky, air cool and fresh, mosquitoes still dozy. I arrive to find the golf course deserted and the club-house locked. What to do – tee off solo without paying or even telling anyone I'm here? As I debate this, a young man with keys in his hand arrives. "Are you here for the tournament?" he asks, clearly surprised to find anyone here before him.

"Uh, no," I squeak, "um, do you think I could, maybe, just go round the course before anyone else gets on?"

"You're by yourself?" He looks incredulous.

"Uh, yes." He quickly regains his composure.

"Well, sure, I suppose so. The tournament doesn't start until nine."

"Oh I'll be long gone by then!" And I'm off.

As I stand alone on the first tee and look up the fairway glistening with dew and crisscrossed by the long shadows of early morning, I think about Sandra and her unshakeable conviction that golf is capable of saving the world. For the first time I see truth in this – if everyone in the world could golf alone at dawn.

I finish my nine holes (eight, in fact: I missed a hole by accident) in just under two hours. One hour and forty-five minutes of vigorous hiking over rugged Canadian Shield terrain, golf bag slung over my shoulder, one hour and forty-five minutes of vigorous swinging (about 120 swings, I figure, including practice swings). I'm wet through my tennis shoes, socks, and lower pantlegs from the heavy dew, wet through my cotton shirt and jacket from perspiration. My leg and shoulder muscles feel stretched and tingly, and I'm smelly and greasy from the confluence of mosquito repellent and sweat. And I'm tired. Damn tired. I vow I'll never again scoff at golf as a sport for the unfit. The mere thought of continuing for another nine holes makes me want to rush to the nearest exit. Plus, I'm ravenous: I'm ready for a heaping bacon-and-egg-and-homefries breakfast.

When I arrive back at the cottage, I'm stunned to find a sumptuous breakfast of eggs, bacon, tomato, cheesebread, and coffee on the table. David has prepared all this – for me. How did he know I'd be starving?

"Well, how did it go?" he asks, as we settle down to our laden plates.

"Well, my swing is loosening up nicely," I say. "And on the 9th hole, I think I had a real breakthrough. It finally feels easier and more fluid and *right* to bring my backswing back maybe six inches more *and* cock my wrists at the top of it. I just felt I had it . . . and a couple of balls on the last hole were just good enough to make me feel that maybe I've progressed . . . a couple of nanomillimetres?"

"And the mosquitoes?" David asks.

"Put it this way," I reply, "Parry Sound mosquitoes certainly contribute to ready golf. But it was worth battling bugs for the experience of playing alone. Alone with my thoughts in the early-morning light. Alone with my swing thoughts, too."

I've got the click. But nine holes is more than enough for this fragile bod.

"I see no good reason to join a golf club," I say to Dianne. "I'm having the time of my life trying out different golf courses. Isn't that supposed to be one of golf's big pluses over, say, tennis? Every course is different?"

Dianne doesn't argue with me. She just invites me to lunch at her golf club, the Toronto Hunt Club. When we were in North Carolina, discussing the pros and cons of taking up golf, Dianne described what was, for her, ultimate bliss. Ultimate bliss was having a drink in midsummer on the spacious front lawn of the Toronto Hunt Club, which overlooks the spectacular Scarborough Bluffs, and gazing out over Lake Ontario.

Well. When it comes to ultimate bliss, Dianne gives you the goods. I drive a long way east on Kingston Road, a utilitarian thoroughfare that like so many mixed business/residential streets in Toronto seems to go on forever. And then suddenly, there are the white gates that Dianne has told me to watch for. I make an abrupt right turn, and in a heartbeat I'm in another world. I descend a wide curving driveway surrounded by generous lawns and lined with huge trees. It ends in a small circular drive, greenery in the middle, at what clearly is the back entrance. I am transported to La Cienega, an ancient hacienda in the highlands of Ecuador I visited a few years ago. Like La Cienega, this is spectacular without being showy, looks comfortably lived in and old but not crumbling. I half expect to see jacaranda or banyan trees, Spanish moss and giant cutleaf philodendron. But remarkably, the trees and greenery that are here – simple Canadian fare like big old oaks and maples, variegated hosta and the like – don't take away from the semi-tropical ambience. It feels lush, gracious, unpretentious. All this, and I hadn't even made it in the back door.

Dianne awaits me on the front lawn, which runs flat and wide and uninterrupted to an abrupt end at an unprotected precipice, the Scarborough Bluffs. The absence of fence or wall gives the effect of gazing out towards infinity. Below and beyond, the vast sea that is Lake Ontario is dead calm, shimmering into a hazy horizon, empty of yachts and even sailboats today, a delirious, delicate palest of blues. "Of course, I ordered this day," Dianne says happily, as we raise a glass. Gracious God, how can I ever go back to Flemingdon now?

But back I do go. It's the last week in June, and Sharon and I get to Flemingdon Park between 12 and 1 P.M., the one time all day, according to the pro shop, that things quiet down. The pro shop is right: we don't have to wait at all.

I was a bit leery about playing at high noon – mad dogs and Englishmen and all that – but the heat isn't as bad as we'd feared, partly because there's a breeze and also because there's a lot of shade on this lovely old course. After a heavy rain early this morning, the Don River is muddy and swollen, the highest Sharon's ever seen it. Parts of the course are sodden; I barely recognize a couple of holes. I remember David's comment about how playing the same golf course is always different. The course is in amazingly good shape, considering its almost-public nature and urban setting. My brief exposure to the Hunt Club has not jaded me! Of course, I haven't *played* it yet . . .

Sharon and I are tailing two elegant men – one about sixty-five, the other about twenty-five. I presume they've been paired up by chance, since their chat is cordial but not chummy and the younger one calls the older one "Mister." They're a pleasure to observe: both good golfers with impeccable manners (Sandra would approve!), both lean and athletic-looking, the older man wearing a dashing riverboat gambler hat, the younger man blond, handsome, and wearing beautifully cut khaki trousers. Both carry their clubs (there are no motorized golf carts at Flemingdon).

I've lost my jitters about the game. And as I relax, my swing is starting to get sloppy. Sandra's instruction is getting a bit fuzzy; I need to go back to the "books" and brush up on my technique. But my new, relaxed attitude means I'm no longer obsessed with seeing how far I can hit the ball. I'm beginning to appreciate the satisfaction of a really good pitch or chip, especially if it lands nicely on the green. For the first time today, I feel I should try using a couple more clubs (I'm still using David's old clubs). I think of clubs like gears on a bicycle. I remember when a three-speed bike was the ultimate two-wheeler; then it was a ten-speed . . . and now? God knows. I have no idea how many gears my comfortable, generic fifteen-year-old bicycle has. What I do know is I don't use any more than five or six of them, and I shift gears more or less by feel. I suspect golf clubs are something the same. I have an aesthetic aversion to industrial-size golf bags stuffed to the limits with clubs and other paraphernalia. They're just plain ugly, as well as ungainly. And I bet most people don't use half the clubs they carry! However, restricting myself to two irons, a pitching wedge, and a putter may be carrying minimalism a bit far.

My sloppy game today involves quite a few worm-burners (one of the terms I've picked up for those dribble-along-the-grass efforts). But I'm still getting at least one really good, straight-down-the-fairway, in-the-air, eighty-to-a-hundred-yard shot per hole. Now that I'm over my jitters and settling into the game, I sense that my standards for myself must rise. This, of course, is the eternal golf trap, which I've been reading about at length in a 1908 golf classic by Arnold Haultain called *The Mystery of Golf*:

> "After all, what leads you on in golf is this. You think a perfect pitch of excellence can be attained. But that pitch of excellence continually recedes the nearer you approach it. . . . Always you can imagine a longer drive, a more accurate approach, a more certain put[t]; never, or rarely ever, do you effect all three at every hole in the course. But all men – who are golfers – always live in hopes of accomplishing them."

But in *my* case, I *will* accomplish these things!

A fellow student in one of Sandra's short-game clinics, hearing that I was a complete beginner, asked me quizzically, "Do you have anyone to play with?" and invited me to join her for a game. I was immensely flattered to be singled out by a relative stranger. Especially since Lauren, a trim, pretty woman somewhere in her forties, is far from a beginner herself. This is her fifth golf summer, and she and her husband play a lot – especially this year, having bought a golf "book" containing discount coupons at courses all over Ontario. "It was a really good deal," Lauren says. "It cost $39.95 and we saved the price of the book on our first round. It forces us to get out and try new courses. We've been all over the place, even spent weekends in a few towns."

This sounds like fun to me – combining golfing with exploring the byways of Ontario. One of Sandra's favourite phrases in the charming golf-boostering talks she delivers in all her clinics is "golf is a lifestyle." I abominate the word "lifestyle" – I'm certain it was invented by a real-estate developer – but I understand what Sandra means by it. And, at this stage of my golf learning-curve (speaking of abominable phrases), buying a golf discount book seems to me to make much more sense than joining a golf club. Get out there and find out what it's all about!

> ## AN ASIDE FROM SANDRA
>
> Loral's throwaway line, "When am I going to have a really bad day?" will come back to haunt her . . . as it does every golfer. I won't spoil her story by saying any more, for the moment!

Lauren and I meet at Oakville Executive, where we are paired with Phil and Doreen, an English couple in their sixties. Doreen is new to the game; Phil is not. I play my usual game: mainly straight-ahead shots, just under a hundred yards, mostly off the ground, but some not, a few terrible shots. When am I going to have a really bad day? I wonder.

Lauren is a very competent player. She has beautiful form, finishing every shot facing the target straight and tall, the posture in which pro golfers are perennially photographed. Lauren has never taken a lesson on the full swing. She's learned on the job, so to speak, strictly from playing with other golfers. But if she had taken lessons, she tells me, "I'd have learned much faster."

The big news of the round for me: On the 6th hole, Lauren lends me her 5-wood, one of her brand-new set of graphite clubs. I'm reluctant to try it, but I'm encouraged by Phil, who says, "Try it! If you never *try* woods, you'll never get used to them."

I rise to the challenge, particularly because I'm facing a huge pond almost directly in front of the tee – and the prospect of losing my ball if I don't hit it at least a hundred yards. The wood will hit it farther, Phil and Lauren assure me. As soon as I pick up the wood, I like it. Yes, the awful memory of that humid Sunday at the Golf Ranch when I pounded Sandra's giant driver time and again into the turf still haunts me. But this wood feels wonderfully light, airy almost. I grip way down the shaft, so that the length doesn't intimidate me, take a few practice shots, and give it a mighty whack. Up, up, up . . . and straight down into the pond. I feel like Kevin Costner on the last hole in *Tin Cup*. I take out another ball, take a couple more practice shots, and *voilà!* – the next one soars over the water. Now that feels good.

From then on, Lauren kindly lends me her 5-wood to tee off with. Until the 9th hole, when Phil goads me into using Lauren's driver. It feels really huge, but I manage to hit the ball. It's the graphite shafts that make all the difference, Lauren says. The pro who sold them to her told her that aluminum – the material her old clubs were made of – is so unforgiving he was amazed she was still standing. "He was right," she adds. "I don't have to work nearly as hard now. And I feel much better after a round: the graphite clubs don't cause nearly as much vibration, so my bones and muscles don't feel rattled."

Phil's wife, Doreen, a tiny, pale woman, is a complete beginner and horribly embarrassed to be playing with strangers. For most of the round she is mute. The one time she speaks to me she says sorrowfully, "Oh, it must come so easily to *you*."

"Not at all," I protest unconvincingly. "You see, I've had a lot of lessons, and . . ."

Phil, paunchy and placid, proves to be a sensitive New Age guy in old-fogey mufti. He quietly encourages Doreen as she shoots her piddlers, never losing patience, offering very little advice and instruction, just gently encouraging her every time she hits the ball. I am impressed. I tell him so. "It's really all about confidence," he replies. "If you think you can, you can. And if you can't, what does it matter? It doesn't matter what the neighbours think." *It doesn't matter what the neighbours think.* I'll try to hang on to that. I may need it.

As for Phil's take on me: he stubbornly refuses to believe that this is only the fifth round of golf I've ever played. And he's serious! Ah, if only Sandra were here.

I cannot contain myself; I telephone Sandra to crow about my progress. It's been three weeks since I've seen her. "Great, Loral!" she sings into the phone. "So why don't you come out to Oakville tomorrow and show me? We'll play a couple of holes with John after my last clinic." We agree to meet at 6 P.M.

I arrive at Oakville as Sandra is finishing up her short-game clinic. She's talking about distance. "A hundred and fifty yards is a very good distance for a woman to hit the ball," she says. "If you can drive that far, concentrate on accuracy – and the short game – instead. *That's* how you're going to bring your scores down. Remember, only 10 per cent of golfers ever break a hundred – and that includes men and women. Putting all your efforts into hitting the ball harder and farther isn't going to help you join that 10 per cent." Sandra's wise words, which the twelve women inhale, do not, of course, apply to her. In recent months she's added an extra twenty yards to *her* drive, bringing her distance up to a pretty consistent 245 yards. She credits her extra distance to a new customized set of clubs with much "whippier" (more flexible) shafts than the ones she had been playing with. Later, I'm treated to one of these spectacular drives during our two holes. It is a thing of beauty – high, straight, gracefully arced, supremely powerful.

The course is packed with after-work keeners on this warm summer evening. Sandra scrutinizes the queue at the first tee. "We can do better than this," she says. "Let's go!" John and I jump onto a cart with her. She whips us round to the 17th tee. It's a 141-yard, par-3 hole. No one in sight. Good. We tee off. I use my 7-iron and hit the ball sixty degrees to the right, about fifty feet. I grimace. But my next shot off the fairway is better. As we approach the green, Sandra notices people behind us. No time to dawdle. We skip putting and hurry on to the 18th tee.

The 18th is the longest hole of the course – par 5, 414 yards. "Try this," Sandra says, handing me her 5-wood. I stand up at the tee, take a deep breath, and hit the ball straight, in a beautiful, high arc. I'm ecstatic. "Gosh," I breathe, "how far do you suppose that went?"

"Well, we'll find out," Sandra says. "C'mon, Loral!" She motions to me as she sets off down the fairway at power-walk pace. John jumps into the cart and drives ahead. "This is 'Tour speed,'" Sandra says, counting aloud as she walks. Every giant step measures one yard. I scramble to keep up.

As I fall into step with her, I count in unison. "One hundred and twenty-seven yards!" we cry as we arrive at my ball. I'm exhilarated. What fun! I hit the next couple of balls with Sandra's 7-iron. I notice quite a difference from David's stiffer, heavier 7-iron. But I whiff a couple of times. "That counts as a stroke,"

Sandra says sternly. "We gotta get over these whiffs!" This is good for me, I tell myself. I've been getting slack during my games, ignoring (and not counting) whiffs. Despite my whiffs, Sandra applauds my practice swings, which just brush the grass. And she remarks favourably on how I keep pace. Clearly, this is very important to her. Ready golf. Don't slow down your playing partners; don't hold up the people behind you.

As we hole out on the 18th green, I ask how many strokes I've taken on this hole. "Ten, maybe?" I suggest. "No," Sandra demurs, "not that many." She mentally reviews the hole and counts eight strokes. I'm impressed with the way she can re-create each shot from tee-off to putting green, whereas I'm so intent on keeping going that I forget almost immediately what I did on my last shot. I resolve to make more of an effort to concentrate. Obviously, Sandra considers this important.

Sandra admires my swing. "You're releasing the club really well now," she says. "I see a *big* difference since I last saw you." Then she adds, "Your swing is good because your attitude is good. You're positive. You're enthusiastic." Sandra Post is well pleased with me. I am on top of the world.

CHAPTER 12

COSMO'S WORLD

Golf is *terra incognita* to my parents and two brothers. So my younger brother, Tom, and his wife, Ann, are mildly bemused when David tells them he wants to send their eight-year-old son, Cosmo, to golf camp this summer. Cosmo is not at all sure about this golf idea Uncle David has cooked up, either. It's a day camp that runs for the first two weeks of July, so Cosmo will come home every evening. But Cosmo has twin ten-year-old sisters and this is the first time ever it has been suggested to him that he spend time apart from them. He calls us three days before the camp begins. "I'm going to try it out for two days, Uncle David," he says soberly. "If I don't like it, I think I'll stay home." I suggest to David that we take Cosmo to a driving range the day before golf camp begins to smooth the way. David and Cosmo agree to this plan.

The city air is dense and oppressive when we pick him up at 9 A.M. The day promises to be unbearable by noon. Cosmo, a beautiful child with intense blue eyes, closely cropped dark hair, and a tall, straight body, is wearing shorts, T-shirt, a Raptors basketball cap, and huge ankle-high black-and-white running shoes. He's carrying the junior-size 6-iron he got free at the Toronto Golf Show last February – which he attended with Uncle David.

We head north of the city about fifty kilometres to the driving range I've been frequenting. As we drive, I tell Cosmo about how I've taken up golf this summer and how much I'm enjoying it. "But I wish I'd started at your age," I say. "It would be a lot easier for me now if I had."

"My sisters really want to take up golf, too, you know," Cosmo says pointedly.

"Yes, I know," I say. "Maybe next year they can. By then, you'll be able to show them how to do it." As I say this, I guiltily realize David and I are reinforcing all the boys'-club clichés about golf by singling out the *boy* in the family for golf lessons.

At the driving range, we buy three small buckets of balls. We line up at the tees, with David in front, Cosmo in the middle, and me behind. We all lather on sunscreen and pull our caps low. The day is hotting up fast.

Cosmo starts whacking away and immediately gets a few balls off the ground. He rocks all over the practice tee on his giant sneakers, jumping off one or both feet every time he hits the ball. He looks like a speeded-up cartoon figure, all legs, feet, and cap flailing about. David counsels him to keep his feet quiet and his head down, and to try not to swing so hard. "That great big heavy club will do the work for you, Cos," he says. I remember an item about kids and golf I've read in one of the little golf classics written by the late Harvey Penick – legendary Texan golf-caddy-turned-teacher. Penick wrote, in effect, "Let the kid have fun, don't overteach; in fact, don't teach much at all, just let the child develop a 'natural' swing." I decide to make it a game. Cosmo and I will have a contest: we'll hit five balls, counting one, two, three, *go*, and see who hits the farthest. I win the first round. We raise the stakes to ten balls. This time Cosmo wins. He's ecstatic. His confidence overflows his sneakers.

As I concentrate on Cosmo, I forget about myself. I just stand up at the tee, sweat pouring down my face and drenching my shirt, and swing like crazy. I think of nothing; I am swing-thought minus. To my surprise, I hit the ball well. Three or four out of five balls are in the air – and they travel beyond the 100-yard mark on the range. Is this what trusting your body is all about?

We bang away for maybe forty-five minutes. When our buckets are empty, David and I tell Cosmo that he's now a golfer. We're sure of this, we say. Cosmo glows. The three of us repair to Country Style Donuts for lunch.

At golf camp, Cosmo makes it through his self-imposed two-day trial period. But only just. After Day One, he reports to Uncle David that it didn't go so well. For starters, he didn't have as much fun as he did with David and me. Second, it was too hot; he got a headache. And "nobody seemed to care." Meaning, perhaps, he didn't get enough attention? This doesn't sound like our Cosmo, a model of sharing all with his sisters, and of waiting his turn. Tomorrow a real game of golf is on the agenda. Cosmo frets that he doesn't know what the game is about; he's afraid he can't do it. Tom comes on the line. No, things weren't terrific today, he says, but Cosmo is going to stick it out until Friday, barring pestilence, famine, or flood. Cosmo agrees, weakly. They hang up.

David calls Cosmo Friday evening. Things have turned around, Cos reports. "Well, I hit it two hundred," he begins, adding soberly, "but that was only when I borrowed my teacher's driver. And I didn't do it *every* time. Only about, maybe, seven times."

I am stunned. Is it possible these numbers mean something other than yards? Well, the practice range is marked "up to 250," Cosmo enlarges. He ticks off his other achievements. "I also learned how to pitch, and I learned how to hit the ball out of sand . . . and, oh yes, I learned how to play a *game* of golf."

David offers golf counsel. "Well, if you can pitch and hit it out of sand and even putt, Cosmo, that's much more important than hitting it a million miles. Often when you hit it really far it goes away off into the woods or somewhere else, nowhere near the hole that you're trying to hit the ball into."

Silence for a moment at the other end of the line. Then a subdued voice whispers, "Do you mean I hit it two hundred *miles*, Uncle David?"

"No, Cosmo. *Nobody* can hit it two hundred miles."

A genuinely perplexed tone now: "But you *said*, 'hit it a million miles.'"

"That was just an expression, Cosmo. What I meant was . . ."

SANDRA REMEMBERS

MY CHILDHOOD LOVE AFFAIR WITH GOLF

Golf entered my life in 1953. In January and February there was nothing to do on my family's fruit farm on the outskirts of Oakville, Ontario, so my parents decided to spend the time in Florida. One day as my father was on his way to watch pro-baseball spring training, he noticed signs for the Orange Blossom Classic LPGA tournament in St. Petersburg. He decided to take me with him.

I was hooked almost from the first moment. Here were *women* playing golf! They were real pioneers: until 1950 there had been no pro women's golf; women just played for trophies, with no money involved. A few women such as the legendary Babe Zaharias decided they wanted to make a living out of golf and formed the LPGA. The women golfers made a real fuss over me and I loved the attention. I also liked the applause from the gallery that I saw the women getting.

One of the women pros, Marilynn Smith, took a special shine to me (she's in her sixties now, living in Dallas, Texas, still playing and teaching golf). Marilynn gave me a ball, a glove, and a tee, and I followed her around the course like a little puppy.

By the time I was seven years old, I considered myself a seasoned golfer. My father was a terrific golfer, and I wanted to do whatever my dad did. During summers back in Canada, we hit a lot of golf balls together. Dad would take me to a driving range almost every evening after he finished work on the farm. And, in January, we'd go back to Florida and watch the women pros. By now, I was no longer behind the ropes: I was on the tee, sitting on Marilynn's golf bag! One day I looked up from my perch and announced to Marilynn and her coach, Elmer Priestkorn, that I intended to be a professional golfer when I grew up. Marilynn, ever the gracious lady, took me at my word at once. But Elmer reminded me that a goal like this meant I'd have to practise a great deal. Well, that didn't faze me one bit. I'd made up my mind, and that was my goal from that day on.

My parents never pushed me. Golf was *my* idea from the start. When I was in my early teens, my mother drove me every morning during the summer holidays to the Trafalgar Golf Club north of Oakville, Ontario, where juniors were welcome to join for twenty-five dollars a year. Whoever won the club championship got free membership so, after my first season playing there, I never had to pay!

My buddies and I used to play fifty-four holes every day – just a bunch of kids going round and round and round. Roy Romaine, the pro at the club, really encouraged us. We loved it when it rained, because everyone else would clear the course. We'd take off our shoes and play in our bare feet.

My father was my only teacher until I turned professional when I was nineteen. He really studied the LPGA – their playing techniques, their swings – and he passed it all on to me. We played together virtually every evening. We'd hide out at his golf club on a green with a bag of balls, practising chipping, pitching, and putting. I wasn't allowed to officially join a golf club until I was eleven. But when I was nine, I said I was eleven, so that I could get on the course. I got away with it because everyone knew that I knew how to play, and that I wouldn't get in anybody's way.

My dad never mollycoddled me. He used some of Tiger Woods' father, Earl's, tough-love techniques. For example, when I did badly and got discouraged and said something like, "I'm no good," my father would agree with me.

"You're right," he'd say.

"I'm not going to make it!" I would wail.

"No, you're not," he would nod soberly. This kind of thing toughened me up and firmed up my resolve. Truth is, though, I never really doubted myself or my goal once I'd set it. I never thought, "Oh God, what if I fail?"

And, as I said, my drive to win was entirely my own. One day on a practice range at Lake Worth, Florida, I decided I wanted to hit a thousand golf balls in one day. My poor dad just shook his head and left me there while he went out to play. When he came back after eighteen holes, I'd hit about eight hundred and fifty balls. My hands were blistered (hands recover really fast: you just put them in epsom salts), but I was determined to finish. And I did. I put away those thousand balls.

Since I loved the game so much, I naturally wanted to be the best. So once I'd won half a dozen amateur titles and there were no more mountains to climb as an amateur, I knew I had to turn pro. I *had* to play on the LPGA Tour . . . and I had to win. There was no alternative. I was nineteen. I hadn't looked back since that day with my dad at the Orange Blossom Classic fourteen years before. And I've never looked back since.

On Monday evening, David and I, and Tom, Ann, Cosmo, and his twin sisters all troop out to the practice range about an hour east of the city, where Cosmo's golf camp is taking place. It's parents' night and the range is chock-a-block with kids and parents whacking away, trying to impress one another. To my annoyance, Ann, Tom, and the two girls – none of whom has ever set foot on a golf course – hit the ball quite well, into the air. Tom hits several soaring shots much farther than anything I've *ever* shot. Ann hits it at least as far as I've hit it. The girls are wildly inconsistent, but get a few good ones away. So does Cosmo.

The real star of the evening, however, is Cosmo's new friend Patrick. Patrick is about as tiny as it is possible for a six-year-old to be. When he swings at the ball, his arms look as long as his entire body. He swings straight back, high in the air, and then straight forward equally high. The ball flies up in the air – not two hundred yards, of course, but at least a hundred yards. And it *soars*.

Patrick is magical. He's utterly uninhibited and slightly out of control in a six-year-old-having-fun sort of way. When he addresses the ball, he stands upon no ceremony. He doesn't stop to centre himself, there is no waggle, he just goes at it. And he has a true swing. David chats with Patrick's doting father, Louis, and learns that Patrick's been playing golf since he was four.

Cosmo's swing doesn't begin to measure up to Patrick's. He's still erratic and undisciplined. But he does hit the ball well several times. How can a ninety-pound eight-year-old or, indeed, a sixty-pound six-year-old, hit the ball a hundred yards?

When Cosmo's golf camp finishes, I invite him to play a game with me. Sandra recommends we go to Mayfield Golf Course, an unadorned public course north of the city, where one of her School of Golf pros teaches juniors. Mayfield is a perfect course for young players and new players. It's laid out in flat countryside against a distant horizon; the clubhouse is a simple snackbar, the trees newly planted, there's nothing to interrupt the view between us and the setting sun.

The past few days have been brutally hot and oppressively humid. Cosmo and I decide that sundown is the most sensible time to go. The course is not busy when we arrive, and the air in this open expanse feels fresh. Cosmo suggests we play "best ball," which he's learned at golf camp. He explains: "We both hit the ball together, and then we go to whichever ball is farthest away and then we both hit from there." Fine. We tee off. I hit my standard ninety-yards-down-the-fairway shot. Cosmo tees off twice, and even his second shot runs along the ground, approximately twenty yards. "I think you're a better golfer than I am, Aunt Loral," Cosmo says, his tone one of simple acceptance. Cosmo faces hard truths straight on.

But things change fast. Cosmo outshoots me almost half the time. When he hits the ball well, in the air, the electricity of his pleasure charges the atmosphere. The best-ball format keeps our game moving at a good clip. It also gives us an opportunity to congratulate each other in turn. I hit a good shot, and Cosmo turns to me, looks me straight in the eye, and says, "Good shot, Aunt Loral!" And then, a stroke or two later, I return the encomium. We move along this way, hitting the ball and complimenting each other, our rhythm that of a minuet.

It is a refreshing, quiet coda to an oppressive day. A few players precede us, a few others overtake us, and finally we are the last two people on the course. We share a sandwich and a drink on a bench on the 4th tee, the sun a golden ball etched behind a cloud. "We never see a sunset like this in the city," Cosmo remarks, adding wistfully: "One of my sisters' favourite things in the whole world is a beautiful sunset."

Our finest hour is on the last putting green we play. It is our sixth hole. Cosmo holes an eight-footer. Then I hole a ten-footer. As the sun sinks below the horizon, a giant orange-purple orb now, Cosmo and I dance around the flag (carefully, Sandra; we did not damage the green), hugging each other as if we were celebrating round a maypole. We are alone, and it's getting dark fast. Suddenly Cosmo says, "It's time to go home." He's right.

On a hot summer's night at dusk, against a swirl of pink and purple clouds and a blood-orange sun, six holes of golf with Cosmo at Mayfield rivals Dianne's ultimate bliss on the Hunt Club front lawn. Much has been written about fathers and sons building bonds through golf. My golf game with Cosmo shows me golf as a way for any adult to spend time with a child. What other sport could Cosmo and I share so successfully? I cannot think of one. I enjoy especially the quiet moments, interspersed with talk, nothing ever forced. Between comfortable silence and chat, we appreciate the evening and the game.

"Just look at the worlds that golf is opening up for you!" Sandra exclaims when I tell her about Cosmo's and my round. She adds, "Now I ask you, Could you have done that with your nephew three months ago?" Sandra is developing a whole new take on the pre-golf and post-golf Loral (with apologies for the pun). She thinks I am blossoming. She says I'm developing a more outgoing, more confident "golf personality." Stuff and nonsense! I say. Who says golf is changing me? I run this notion by a few friends. Stuff and nonsense! they say. Why, you've always been confident and outgoing, Loral. But this golf thing, well, it's certainly changing your *life* . . .

SANDRA TALKS ABOUT JUNIOR GOLF

I started playing golf at the age of five when my dad took me to an LPGA tournament in Florida and I fell in love with the game. That's how most PGA and LPGA players start playing golf – through a parent's influence when they're very young, usually between the ages of three (Tiger Woods) and eight (Nancy Lopez) or ten (Barb Bunkowsky-Scherbak).

You're never too young to start golf. A cut-down club is important at the beginning. A club of your own that's the right size for you is something a young golfer can control. You'll learn about the responsibilities that go with having your own club: not swinging the club near someone, never throwing it, not leaving it behind and losing it. Club manufacturers now make junior golf-club sets in a wide variety of price ranges. But one club is enough to start with.

When you're very young, you can start golf at a public practice range, where there are no age restrictions. A baseball grip is fine for kids, so long as the child places his or her hands close together. Try to help your child learn to swing in balance. It's natural for high-energy kids to take a running start or to pirouette after they hit the ball, but maintaining balance is key to developing a good golf swing. It's natural, too, for children to have very short attention spans. So it's important to keep golf simple and fun. Playing mini-golf, for example, is lots of fun and will help children with putting later on.

Getting children onto a golf course can be a problem because of age restrictions. This is something we must all work towards changing in golf. Part of the reason for the reluctance to allow young golfers onto courses is fear on the part of owners that they will damage the course. It is, of course, the responsibility of adults to teach young golfers the etiquette of the game.

But things are changing fast in the 1990s in the world of junior golf. Tiger Woods' phenomenal success at such a young age has had a tremendous effect. Golf camps for juniors and junior tours are in huge demand, and they're growing fast. Some examples:

• The LPGA works with the United States Golf Association (USGA), the Girl Scouts of the United States, and Crayola Brand sponsoring golf clinics and learning programs for young players.

• The PGA of America sponsors many youth golf programs. Among them is one partnered with Renée Powell, an African-American pro from Ohio who was on the LPGA Tour in the 1960s and 1970s (Renée and I were roommates on the Tour and have remained close friends). Powell's Youth Golf Cadre Program introduces disadvantaged inner-city children, who wouldn't normally get a chance to hit golf balls, to golf.

• The Swedish Golf Federation, directed by Pia Nilsson, has done a remarkable job of building golf awareness in Sweden and producing a torrent of world-class players in a country with a climate no more clement than Canada's and with about a third our population (to name a few of Sweden's stars: Jesper Parnevik, Annika Sorenstam and her sister Charlotta, Liselotte Neumann, Helen Alfredsson).

• And here in Canada, the Royal Canadian Golf Association (RCGA) sponsors a very successful junior golf program called Future Links. Since its inception in 1996, more than ten thousand children from all across Canada have taken part in the program.

CHAPTER 13

RIDING HIGH

I watched my first LPGA major this weekend, the U.S. Open. Can it be only three months since I had to grit my teeth to gear myself up to watch the Masters? It feels like another era.

This is the first time I've seen the storied Nancy Lopez, long beloved by her devoted fans. When Sandra won back-to-back LPGA Dinah Shore Championships in 1978 and 1979, Nancy was the bright younger star who challenged her, just as Sandra had challenged the older Kathy Whitworth a decade earlier. Nancy is forty now. As I watch her over the final two days of the Open, I understand completely why the crowd loves her. She is the soul of graciousness; she is controlled, as she must be, but her emotions play across her face like a breeze passing over daisies in a meadow. She emanates *simpatìa*. The American TV network grinds on and on about Nancy's "balance of family and career." Certainly her motherhood-and-apple-pie image is part of her appeal: she has three children; she's married to baseball star Ray Knight; and she's weathered a very public battle of the bulge, and at the moment is photogenically trim.

The Open ends in a classic *mano-a-mano* struggle between the older crowd darling, who has paid her dues and desperately wants the crown, and the frisky, younger terrier, whom no one really knows, nipping at her heels. Nancy has never won the U.S. Open, and this is considered one of her last serious chances at the title. English player Alison Nicholas is thirty-five but seems younger, partly because of her size – she's barely five feet tall – and partly, perhaps, because she is not yet a household name among golf aficionados. Alison plays a cool-headed, utterly focused game. No emotions playing across *her* face. Until the very end, that is, when she wins in a white-knuckle putting contest with Nancy. Nancy cracks on a fifteen-foot putt that could have forced a playoff, and Alison wins the title. And she lets her emotions fly at last, in a whoop of victory.

I talk with Sandra after the tournament, and she agrees that Alison won it fair and square with her short game. "Nancy's older, and it just gets harder," Sandra says, meaning that the concentration, the cool, the nervelessness that good putting takes gets more difficult with age.

In her victory speech, Alison proves herself to be a class act. She gives Nancy her full due and shows no resentment whatsoever of the gallery, which has clearly favoured Nancy throughout the Open. After Alison's win, the cameras shift to a scoring tent, where the players are sitting at a long table having cold drinks just before the awards ceremony. Alison is hugging Nancy and consoling her. This scene blows David away. For two days he has cheered lustily for Nancy and, when she loses, he sheds a few tears. And now, as he noisily blows his nose, he sees this display of sportsmanship and camaraderie. "Look at that!" he exclaims. "You would *never* see something like that in men's professional golf. After a major championship like the Open, they'd all be locked into their own private egotistical testosterone bubbles!"

Lots of golf nuances still pass me by, and I'll probably make many more bloopers, such as feigning interest in a "par-9" hole. But I think I'm an insider now. I thoroughly enjoyed this tournament; I was right into it, like a mud-covered pair of golf shoes. I found all the women interesting, I could follow all the play and 90 per cent of the commentary and, as Sandra emphasizes to her students, both male and female, one can relate to women professionals in a way that you cannot to the male pros, who play utterly unattainable games and rake in stratospheric sums doing so.

I invite Dianne to play a round with me at Oakville Executive. "I'll book us for nine holes," I say.

"But, Loral, you just get warmed up on the first nine!" Dianne replies.

"I've never played eighteen holes," I splutter, "and I'm not at all sure I want to."

"Oakville is a short course, isn't it?" she persists.

"Yes, but . . ." I book us for eighteen holes.

We're paired with Roseanna and Teena, both in their twenties. "Rosey" and "Teen," as they quickly become as we settle into our round, are wearing scuffed tennis shoes, T-shirts emblazoned with Citytv and Rotterdam beer logos, and trendy *Postcards from the Edge* sunglasses that set off *l'animal* hair. Rosey is the elder and more rounded of the two; she's about thirty pounds overweight, most of it settling around her hips. Teena has beestung lips and a tight-fitting T-shirt, but her self-described "big butt," riding within white denim shorts with a zipper that refuses to stay more than halfway up, mars the symmetry a bit. I've never before envisioned Dianne as a well-cared-for middle-aged matron, but in this context that is precisely what she looks like. With her petite figure, subtly streaked dark hair, fuchsia shirt – which she has handpainted – matching Bermuda shorts, and immaculate golf shoes, she could be Martha Stewart.

Teen tees up with self-conscious flourish. She wields a large driver. The ball dribbles five yards down the fairway. Rosey's drive is marginally better. Dianne and I groan. "I think it's going to be a long day," I whisper. Teen saunters down the fairway, golf bag slung over her shoulder ("Oh, it's not heavy. I'm trying to get weight off my butt. See?"). She appears in no hurry to hit her second shot.

Eventually, she dribbles the ball a few feet more. She and Rosey chat for several minutes before she hits it a third time. This shot travels about fifty yards.

By the time we make it to the first green, my blood pressure has risen. I fret about dislodging Dianne from her idyllic golf haven on the Scarborough Bluffs.

On the 3rd tee, Teen drives the ball two hundred yards, in a spectacular, soaring arc. So does Rosey. And I, after a respectable start on holes one and two, do a bump-and-run.

Rosey and Teen are marvellously consoling to me.

When I watch Teen now, her practice swings look deliciously fluid and loose-jointed, in contrast to my tight little, right little ones. Funny, they'd looked utterly out of control on the first two tees. Teen follows these drives with equally loose-jointed, nonchalant putting. Just when I least expect her to, she holes out.

Rosey gives Teen tender counsel every step of the way. After a while, Dianne and I start to tune in. What we overhear borders on excellent pro instruction. It goes far beyond keeping your head down and your feet and lower body still. Rosey squares up Teen's stance, counsels her on which club to use when, explains when she must take a penalty, and uses terminology like "dogleg to the right." Teen's magnificent drives don't occur on every tee, but they do on two out of three, even if they aren't always on target. I note the free and easy movement around her shoulders, the effortless way she seems to swing.

On the 6th hole, with a huge water hazard just off the tee, a couple of young studs catch up to us. They give Teen a hard time when she drops her drive into the pond. Teen takes a big breath, dangerously swelling her T-shirt, and retorts that this is her first time on a golf course and she's doing the best she can. She swiftly adds a sharp refusal to let them play through. On the next green, I timidly ask Teen if this is, indeed, her first time on a golf course. She looks at me as if I'm mad. "Are you kidding? This is only the third time I've been out *this* year. But I've been playing off and on for three years now. I took lessons before I started playing at the Etobicoke community centre."

As for Rosey, her dad is a scratch golfer. He took her golfing constantly when she was between the ages of ten and fifteen, and taught Rosey all he knew. "He taught me my swing and I've never lost it," Rosey says modestly. "But I'm married now, so

I don't get out so much." I confide that *I* didn't take up golf until I was fifty-three.

"Oh really?" she replies. I am eager to add that *that* was barely two months ago. But the rejoinder I am waiting for, something along the lines of "but surely *that* can't have been long ago," is not forthcoming.

Rosey and Teen smoke cigarillos between holes. Between the 9th and the 10th holes they grab large beers in the clubhouse and swig them on the 10th and 11th tees. This helps their swings, they giggle. I'm forced to agree. Dianne and I do not grab food or drink between the 9th and 10th holes. It's a hot, still day and I'm flagging fast. I find it difficult to concentrate and I feel slightly dizzy. Somewhere around the 13th tee, Teen, too, notices the heat. Rosey advises her to "air out your armpits. It'll relax you, hon. You're getting too tense." The four of us stand with our arms straight out like scarecrows and slowly waggle them up and down. It has a wonderfully soothing effect. I make a mental note to remember this wise golf tip: *Air out your armpits.*

As for my game, I claim two firsts on this round: on the 2nd hole, I chip into the hole from the fringe, a distance of about twenty-five feet. This is called a "kingsmith," Dianne tells me as she congratulates me. And I par the 17th hole – all 103 yards of it. I'm happy that Dianne, my first golf mentor, is with me to witness this feat.

Otherwise, I play my usual spotty game. Eighteen holes *is* too much for me, especially through the heat of the day. And Rosey and Teen's futzing around holds us up. Plus, the course is crowded and the people in front of us delay us. In the end, the round takes four hours, an hour longer than the posted round time. Sandra's words reverberate in my ears: *ready golf!* I couldn't agree more. This slow play wrecks all sense of momentum and rhythm. I lose my concentration and find it impossible to keep track of my score. Dianne tells me this is normal when you haven't played long. "It's partly because you're hitting so many shots. You'll find that when you're closing in on par it's not hard at all to concentrate." Too true. I had no trouble at all documenting my par 3 on the 17th.

On the last hole, I hit a magnificent drive. Magnificent for me – well over a hundred yards. As I triumphantly set up to hit my second shot, dreaming of parring this par-5 hole, Dianne has a second piece of advice: "Don't try to 'kill'

SANDRA TALKS ABOUT THE TRADITIONS OF THE GAME

THE DRESS CODE

The dress code is a very important part of golf tradition. Dressing properly is a form of discipline and respect for the game. When people dress sloppily, it's reflected in the way they play the game, and the way they treat the golf course and their playing partners.

Jeans, sweatpants, cutoffs, and untailored T-shirts are not acceptable anywhere except the public driving range. Even public and municipal courses restrict, prohibit, or frown upon such clothing.

When you play at a private club, you can always call the pro shop to see exactly what rules apply. But if you wear a shirt with a collar and sleeves, and tailored pants or Bermuda shorts to the top of the knee, you will be accepted anywhere.

Golf shoes are not strictly required by most clubs. But golf shoes do help ground you, so if you intend to play golf regularly, you should invest in a comfortable pair of golf shoes that provide good support to your feet and ankles. When you play eighteen holes of golf, you walk five to six miles, so good shoes are worth the investment.

---

the ball. The hardest shot in golf is the second one, after you've hit a good drive. You're thinking, 'If I hit another one like that drive, I'll be on the green.' And then you top it, or scull it, or commit some other horrible indignity on the ball." I listen tight – then top the ball. It runs along the ground about twenty yards.

Rosey and Teen are marvellously consoling.

Sandra and I play another early-evening, post-clinic round at Oakville Executive. It's warm but not sticky, no wind, and the course is infused with the long shadows and deep yellow light of the end of a summer's day. And a bonus: a purple-and-gold-streaked sky with an orange-ball sunset. "Why doesn't everyone play golf at this hour?" I ask Sandra.

SANDRA'S POINTERS ON THE TEE

• Don't drag your cart onto the tee. Bring only the club you're using to tee off with.

• *When your playing partner tees off:* Stand at the side of the tee, facing your partner but behind the teed ball. This way you're out of her peripheral vision and will not distract her. Plus you can watch her ball to see where it lands.

• *On the first tee:* This is the most intimidating shot you're going to make all day, because you're in front of the clubhouse and everyone is watching you (or you *think* everyone is watching you!). Try to block out everyone else and focus on your shot. Take a couple of deep breaths, go through your pre-shot routine — don't rush it — then let it fly.

• *The tee markers:* You cannot tee up anywhere you wish to on the tee. Tee up between the tee markers or behind them (up to two club lengths behind, but no farther). If you tee up between the markers, you are permitted to stand with your *feet* outside the tee markers as long as your ball is inside the markers. And you cannot tee up in front of the tee markers. You incur a penalty of two strokes if you do and must then re-tee the ball correctly.

"It's money," she replies. "People don't want to pay for a full round and only be able to get a few holes in. But most courses have twilight rates."

When we played our two holes together a couple of weeks ago, my principal memory is of Sandra pacing out my 127-yard drive and applauding my positive attitude. This time she's tougher with me: she dispenses with the cheerleading and goes to town on my game. She's in teacher mode: I receive a refresher course in rules of the game, etiquette, and swing technique, and a primer on course strategy – where to place my shots depending on the terrain of the golf course, and how to *try* to think one shot ahead.

I tee off badly and continue poorly for a couple of holes. Sandra weathers my bad play, apparently taking no notice, encouraging me to carry on, get on with the game. Then, independent of Sandra, I remember my wristcock. And I start getting the ball off the ground. Sandra pounces. *Now* she tells me what to do, reinforcing what I'm doing right. This is key to Sandra's teaching technique. She never says,

GOLF COURSE STRATEGY FOR BEGINNERS

SANDRA'S STRATEGY FOR NEW GOLFERS ON A PAR-4 HOLE

1. Tee-off Shot: Tee markers can encourage you to misalign your shot if you are not careful. Do *not* automatically tee up square to the tee markers. Angle away from trouble.

2. First and Second Shots: Remember that your practice swing (and you should take one on every shot!) should brush the grass. If your lie is not good, place your ball on a tuft of grass; and if you get completely frustrated, use a tee on the fairway and whichever club you are most comfortable with. Aim both these shots down the centre of the fairway, to avoid the trees, the pond, and the sand bunker.

3. Third Shot: Aim towards the widest part of the green.

4. Fourth Shot: Aim at a three-foot circle around the hole.

"You're doing this, this, and this wrong." Instead she says, "Try this." She shows you what to *do*, instead of dwelling on what you're not doing.

On the next tee, Sandra braces me with some swift pointers. Now she makes me abide by the rules, including rules I'm not aware of. No exceptions. If I tee off badly, I tee off badly – no mulligans. On one tee-off, I hit

my ball into water. "Your next shot is your third shot," she reminds me. *Stroke plus distance.* The only slack she cuts me is occasionally giving me a better lie for my ball. This is against the rules, of course. But anything that makes the ball easier to hit, Sandra considers fair play for a beginner. Once, when I was practising at the Golf Ranch and having problems getting the ball off the ground, she advised me to practise off a tee. Don't worry that most shots in a real golf game are not teed up, she said. What a good swing is all about is *confidence*, and you need to see ball after ball after ball going into the air to get your confidence up.

I'm so keyed up knowing *I'm playing golf with Sandra Post* that I forget to keep track of my score. Again and again, Sandra gently but firmly brings me back to it. *Concentrate!* Sometimes this is gratifying as well as humbling: on two par-3 holes, I hole out in five strokes. Sandra points out that this is called a double-bogey – which puts me on the scoreboard! A recognized score in other words – unlike, say, ten strokes on a par 5.

On the 5th hole she tackles golf-course strategy. Instead of aiming for the hole, which is over a small hill to the right and through some trees, Sandra tells me to aim for the centre of the fairway: "You need to lay up well for a clean shot to the pin." To accomplish this shot, I have to be punctilious about alignment, a basic I've been having a lot of problems with. She gives me pointers: "Close your clubface like so . . . move your body around so that you're square to the target." I do so – and, to my delight, find myself in a better position for my last shot to the green than Sandra's position.

SANDRA TALKS ABOUT THE TRADITIONS OF THE GAME

THE IMPORTANCE OF ETIQUETTE

Golf comes from a long and honourable tradition, and behaviour is important; indeed, it is an integral part of the game. When new players take up golf, it's important they understand golf etiquette. Proper behaviour during a round of golf means being courteous to others and respectful of the golf course. It means raking the bunkers, repairing divots, letting people play through, and keeping quiet when another person is making a shot.

When golfers don't respect the traditions and etiquette of the game, you see terrible abuse of golf courses and other players. You see unrepaired divots on the fairway, players hitting balls close to you and not yelling "fore," people throwing golf clubs, and golfers dragging their spikes on the green. When things like this happen, it takes an enormous amount away from the game.

Sandra explains the difference between a fairway bunker and a greenside bunker – a distinction that has not occurred to me. The technique she teaches in her short-game clinic relates to a greenside bunker, she adds. When you hit out of a fairway bunker, which by definition is a long way from the green, you use a full swing.

And she reinforces rules and points of etiquette that I've heard or read but somehow haven't registered. Such as:

- You can *never* pick up your ball when it's not on the green. Not even when you're planning to use a putter from the fringe of the green.
- To speed up the game, set your clubs off the side of the green leading to the next tee. And keep your clubs together; don't leave one club lying on the side of the green: it's easy to forget it.

Later in our round, Sandra tells me about an incident earlier today. The sand bunker she teaches in is parallel to the first hole. Occasionally, balls travel dangerously close to her students. Today, a player came over to retrieve an out-of-bounds ball that had startled her class. "You should have called 'fore!'" Sandra told the player sharply.

SANDRA EXPLAINS WHITE, RED, AND YELLOW STAKES

White Stakes: White stakes on a golf course mean that the area outside them is out of bounds. The penalty is "stroke plus distance." If you hit your tee shot out of bounds, you simply hit a second ball off the tee; and this second shot counts as your *third*, because of the stroke plus distance rule.

Red and Yellow Stakes: Red and yellow stakes or lines indicate the boundaries of water hazards. Lateral water hazards are defined by red stakes or lines; the rest by yellow stakes or lines. If a ball is in or lost in a water hazard, the player, under penalty of one stroke, may: a) play a ball as nearly as possible at the spot from which the original ball was last played; or b) drop a ball behind the water hazard, keeping the point at which the original ball last crossed the water hazard between you and the hole. There are also ball-drop areas and local rules regarding environmentally sensitive areas that have been defined as lateral water hazards. New golfers find these water-hazard rules difficult to learn.

You *may* hit from inside red or yellow stakes, if you honour the following guidelines:

1. Take only one club with you (not your golf bag or cart).
2. Do not take a practice swing or ground your club.

If you're playing with a more experienced player, you can always ask your partner for advice about the various options open to you.

To her shock, he replied, "If I hit you, that's *your* problem!"

"A golf ball is a lethal weapon," Sandra says. "On the Tour I saw a golf ball hit someone who was in the gallery on the head, and, let me tell you, it was terrible. I've seen an eye put out! And the amount of blood from a head wound. . . . If a golf ball hits you on the side of your temple" – she shows me the place – "it can kill you.

"This is the public course for this area, so new golfers gravitate here," she continues. "And a lot of them have no idea about the traditions and etiquette of the game.

SANDRA TALKS ABOUT READY GOLF FOR NEW GOLFERS

• *Learn when to pick up the ball:* Golfers get lost in their own inner game — immersed in whatever their goal is today, whether it's breaking a hundred or making par or birdie on a particular hole. So remember, if you're playing with a group that's more advanced than you are, no one will care how badly you play, *if* you keep up with them. Learn when to pick up your ball and move on in order to keep the game moving and not hold up other players. And be ready to play when it's your turn. When your partners say "you're away" (meaning you're farthest from the hole so you play first), play quickly.

• *Let people play through:* Golf etiquette is about consideration for other people. There are three groups of "other players" to be considerate of. The first group are your playing partners. If you are playing badly or if you are a new golfer and your partners are more advanced, be ready to pick up your ball if you are lagging behind.

The second group is the group in *front* of you. So long as you keep up with them, you need never worry about the third group, the one behind you. Think about it: The group behind you gauges its play to how fast you're moving. They don't have any choice! So if you keep up with the group in front of you, you know you're not holding up the pace of the course unless *no one* is in front of you. In this case, if your group is playing slower than the one behind you, etiquette demands that you wave them through.

• *Learn to continuous putt:* New golfers often 3-, 4-, or 5-putt each green. Putting and marking, putting and marking strictly according to the rules, takes *such* a long time. So it's very important to continuous putt until you tap the ball in (avoiding your partners' lines), in order to speed up the game.

• *When it's your turn, be ready to hit the ball:* Women have a reputation for being slow players — although the latest statistics show that men are slower than women. But the stereotype still exists, so women have to try to dispel it. Learn to prepare in advance. As you approach your shot, check your lie and angle, as well as wind and distance. Then, when it's your turn, be ready to hit the ball.

> *Don't get hung up on the rules:* When you're beginning golf, you don't need to know a great number of rules. All you need to know are a few basics.
>
> The important thing to remember is to keep moving. Learn when to pick up your ball and move on. Don't stand upon ceremony. Play on!

"I just hate to see people being rude on the course, ignoring things like white stakes, and the worst: hitting the ball dangerously. This is *not* a snobbish thing. I'm very happy about the way golf is attracting so many new players. But I love this game so much, and I have great respect for its traditions."

We play six holes before the light goes. As we head for the clubhouse, there is dew on the greens. Ah, what a lovely game.

Back to Flemingdon Park. I'm coming to think of Flemingdon as my default course – when I don't make special arrangements, I automatically revert back to it. This is my fourth round at Flemingdon, more rounds than I've played at any other course. I play for the second time with Sharon and her friend Jan, an Australian-Canadian, also in her early fifties.

The pro shop teams us up with a guy called Bill. Bill looks like a throwback to the 1950s, right down to his ancient, desperately scuffed golf bag and clubs. He's about fifty-five, with thick, very black, slightly oiled (Brylcreem?) hair. His face is dominated by heavily framed black glasses that look like no glasses styled since 1959. The only thing in Bill's entire outfit that doesn't look like something bought at an estate sale is his cell phone, which rings on the 6th tee.

Bill is a classic Type-A personality. This is the first summer he's golfed in twenty years, he confides. He gave up the game for many years because he wasn't hitting well, and he couldn't stand playing when he wasn't hitting well. Bill quickly proves himself to be a much better player than Jan, Sharon, or me. And as the round continues, he becomes more and more agitated by the foursome in front of us. It's a convivial group of women in their sixties, and they are dawdling unconscionably. From two hundred yards away, the four of us can clearly see that they're chatting up a storm – smack in the middle of the fairway. And they are *very* bad golfers, plus they know nothing about etiquette. When we're breathing down their necks on a par-3 hole, they fail to wave us through, as etiquette dictates. Jan, a competent golfer who has been playing for seven years, is almost as choked about this as is Bill.

All of which conspires to put off Bill's entire rhythm, he sputters. Mine too – but Bill is so close to meltdown I find it easier to bear than I would have without him. He's our safety valve, blowing off steam for the rest of us. Finally, on the 5th fairway, Bill corners a maintenance worker on a ride-on mower and commands him to drive ahead and tell the women to hurry up.

As I go round Flemingdon's nine holes, I am sanguine about not doing particularly well. Unlike my first hubris-filled round with Sharon five weeks ago, I no longer dispute the fact that she is much better than I am. And Jan is the best of us all. So I quietly go along, playing my own game as I have been taught to do, averaging double-par on each hole. And as I do this, the nanomillimetre principle is noiselessly at work. Jan and Sharon generously note I'm consistently hitting farther on the fairway, that my putting is improving, and that I'm hitting – *not* hitting, rather – fewer whiffs. Now that I'm getting to know Flemingdon, I take pains to play smarter. I put to use some of Sandra's instruction about "course strategy." Remembering that in the past I've lost two or three balls in the stream on the 6th hole, I avoid it this time by hitting to the right. I take more time with my alignment and, as a result, aim more consistently. And I no longer blindly aim for the pin.

And then I am unobtrusively going about my business on the 8th hole, a par 4 (245 yards), when I suddenly realize I'm on the green. I'm four feet away from the hole, in three strokes. "Omigosh," I say, half to myself, "if I make this putt, I'll have a par 4."

Bill overhears me. "You can do it!" he says. "But it requires a good heft, because it's uphill and the green breaks a bit to the right. So aim very slightly to the left." I follow Bill's instruction to the letter. And I hole it.

The rush this gives me is almost shameful. There I am, kidding myself that I'm just plodding along, doing the best I can. But the truth is, in my heart of hearts I

SANDRA TALKS ABOUT ETIQUETTE ON THE GREEN

• *You and your putter only, please:* Only you and your putter are welcome on the green. Never bring your golf bag or pullcart onto the green (or, obviously, drive a golf cart onto the green).

• *Be gentle with the flag:* Treat the flag with respect. Remove it carefully and lay down the flagstick *gently* – well back from the hole – so as not to damage the green. Then replace it just as carefully, so that you do not damage the cup and its edges.

• *Tread lightly on the green:* Walk carefully on the green – don't drag your feet! And tap down spike marks – including those left behind by other players – before you leave the green. This is a courtesy to other players, and will make everyone's game a lot more enjoyable.

• *Repair the green:* To repair a ball mark on the green, gently press the grass forward towards the middle of the mark with a divot repairer or tee. Then tap it down with your shoe or your putter. Pressing forward on the grass like this aerates the roots, and the ball mark will mend itself overnight. If you pull up on the roots instead of pressing forward gently, it will kill them. And if you do nothing, the ball mark will quickly turn into a dead, brown spot, marring the green.

• *Honour your partner's putting line:* Be aware of other players' "putting line" (the intended line from their ball to the hole). Never walk across it or, indeed, anywhere between a person's ball and the hole. Walk *around* it, on the outside.

• *Attend the pin:* If your playing partner is too far away to clearly see the hole, you should attend the pin (also called the flagstick). As soon as your partner strokes the putt, remove the pin, because if the ball hits the pin while it's in the hole, it's a two-shot penalty.

• *Let your partner go first:* If your playing partner is closer to the pin than you are but is still *off* the green (on the fringe or in a greenside bunker), it is courteous to let her play first.

want to do better, *much* better. And when I do it, the adrenalin rushes in. Yes! *This* is what it's all about.

To cap my triumph, I get my lowest score yet, 66, a mere thirty-one strokes over par. Forty-two fairway shots and twenty-four putts – and I was forced to hurry putts several times because the course was so crowded. So I figure I *could* have made, say, eighteen or twenty putts under ideal conditions. When I tell David, he seems genuinely impressed. "You parred a 245-yard hole?" he cries. "You're so far ahead of me!" This is not true, of course, but I like hearing him say it. He adds, "Once you've got the feeling of a par 4, you know you can do it again."

Jan scores 51, Sharon 57. Funny, I no longer suspect their scores! Sharon says she did not take any mulligans on this round – except off the first tee, which she decrees to be acceptable.

On the second last weekend in July, David and I watch the British Open being played at the Royal Troon Golf Course in Scotland. David's predictions about Tiger Woods after the Masters way back in April ("he won't win tournament after tournament . . .") are proving more and more prescient. Tiger thrills everyone with a record-low score of 64 on Saturday. And then, on Sunday, his putting falls apart and he blows himself out of the tournament when he fails to negotiate a couple of treacherous bunkers.

And these bunkers *are* treacherous, verging on the impossible. They look like Second World War dugouts, as steep as the cliffs of Dover and so deep the players can barely see over their rims (correctly called "lips" in golf lingo). The entire Royal Troon course makes American championship courses look designed for overindulged kids. "Rugged" is the obvious adjective; perhaps bleak should precede it. The fairways would make a perfect setting for *King Lear*: treeless, wind-swept, an autumnal yellow-brown where grass manages to grow, hard and grey as granite in the bare patches in between. As for the rough, David calls it "serious spinach" – somewhere between ankle-deep and knee-high. To compete well on British courses, American pros, who have been pampered on manicured courses groomed and watered to a fare-thee-well, often spend long weeks practising on them.

David gives me a quick primer on the classic Scottish-links course. They're seaside courses that hug the coastline, he says. They were designed by artisans, following the contours of the dune; not by fancy landscape architects specializing in golf. Their layout tends to be the same: the front nine holes run one way, parallel to the shoreline; and the back nine run alongside, back to where they started. So, links courses are all long and narrow, and when you finish your first nine you can't catch your breath – and a pint – in the clubhouse as you can at most North American courses, which are laid out with the 9th and the 18th holes ending there. "In Scotland, you're out there for eighteen holes, period," says David. Scottish golf is not for sissies.

Royal Troon's clubhouse is a sharp contrast to the Congressional Country Club's white palace on the hill overlooking the golf course in Bethesda, Maryland, where the U.S. Open was played five weeks ago. Royal Troon's clubhouse is small, and low-key. The only thing that raises it above ordinary are the tastefully small, classical pillars at the front entrance. The message is obvious: American golf is for millionaires; British golf is for the people.

I'm developing an armchair love affair with British golf. I'm fascinated by Andy's description of the Irish courses he played last month, courses with wild, romantic names like Ballybunion, Lahinch, Tralee, Killarney. Negotiating these courses is like hacking your way through a Northern Hemisphere jungle, Andy reports. There are no paths, no signs, no hole numbers. When you tee off, you frequently have no idea where the green is, let alone the next hole. One storied hole on the Lahinch links has a blind green over a hill. Every day a team of barrel-chested Irishmen moves a rock half the size of Rio de Janeiro's Sugarloaf Mountain in line with the flag over the hill, to give players some idea where to aim! The only sane or, indeed, possible way to navigate these courses, Andy advises, is to hire a caddy who functions as your guide and trailbreaker.

Such descriptions render me weak-kneed with desire to play a romantic Scottish or Irish course. A couple of books I've been reading add to the mystique of Celtic golf: the 1970s classic *Golf in the Kingdom*, set on the mythical Links of Burningbush, "an innocent stretch of heather and grassy dunes" on Scotland's shores, a book I found slightly bogus but infused with an alluring, wild-eyed aura

SANDRA TALKS ABOUT THE CHALLENGE OF BRITISH GOLF

I love golfing in Britain because I'm a purist. This is where golf began, and this is the way golf used to be. Forget carpetlike, impeccably groomed courses. Expunge all memories of the perfect lie. On many courses in Scotland, England, Wales, and Ireland, you hit the ball . . . and then you go looking for it! Combine rugged terrain (animal tracks in the bunkers; knee-deep rough; rocky ground) and harsh weather (rain coming off the sea at right angles; winds so ferocious you can barely stand up) and what do you have? The challenge of British and Irish golf. It's an achievement simply to finish your round.

And when you do finish, you feel a true sense of accomplishment.

nonetheless (as you'd expect from author Michael Murphy, founder of California's Esalen Institute, cradle of the Human Potential Movement). More to the point, and much more grounded, are the writings of Henry Longhurst, the legendary British golf writer and commentator, who died in 1978. Longhurst was less a romantic than a purist about his beloved sport. He subscribed to a minimalist ideal: toting seven or eight clubs, tops, in a "drainpipe" bag you can easily sling over your shoulder; and its corollary, always walking the golf course. Longhurst despised what he called "electrified trollies," electric golf carts to us. And he was a man after Sandra's heart: he abominated slow play. He constantly railed on in his columns about the way slow play destroys the natural, pure rhythms of the game. And Americans are by far the worst offenders in this department, he wrote.

On a recent round at Flemingdon, I observed a lean young man who cut a dashing figure carrying the ultimate drainpipe bag, slung at a rakish angle across one shoulder. Together, he and the bag looked smashing. The bag, made of heavy canvas, was a classy shade of khaki, and considerably slimmer than *my* cheap, synthetic drainpipe bag. It was the golf bag of my dreams.

As for golf in Britain: I will continue to nurture from afar my love affair with remote Scottish and Irish courses. I love the *idea* of them: their wildness, their unkemptness, their proximity to the raging sea. Surely this is what golf is about, at its core. Wandering barely charted links by the sea, lonely as a cloud, slim canvas bag carelessly slung over one shoulder . . . A vision several galaxies removed from my original image of fat, overpaid men stuffed into electric carts.

CHAPTER 14

GLEN ABBEY

It's the last week in July now, and David and I have tickets to the LPGA du Maurier Classic being held at the Glen Abbey Golf Club in Oakville. Glen Abbey is probably the most famous public golf course in Canada. It's home to the Canadian Golf Hall of Fame (Sandra is a member, of course), the men's Canadian Open (although not this year), and the Royal Canadian Golf Association (RCGA). It was designed in 1977 by Jack Nicklaus for professional tournaments, so it's laid out to accommodate huge galleries of fans.

Sandra is commenting on the Classic for CTV. She's been touting this tournament to her students all summer. The du Maurier Classic, which started out in the early 1970s as La Canadienne and is, in every respect, the Canadian Women's Open, has never before been played at Glen Abbey, she points out. So this is something special – a major LPGA tournament in your backyard, a golden opportunity to see up close the best women players in the world.

David is super-keen to attend. He's always been a big fan of women's professional golf. It's much more human-scale than men's pro golf, he says. The women are not infused with the giant egos the men have, and you can learn from watching women pros in a way you cannot from the men. The men's game is exciting to watch, but it's far beyond anything any of us mere mortals can ever aspire to.

We spend our first day at the Classic on Tuesday, practice day. From the moment we arrive, I'm impressed by the size and slickness of the tournament's organization. Everywhere we are greeted by cheerful volunteers, wearing black straw hats and red-and-black outfits. Yellow ropes line the fairways, but the women pros casually walk around the grounds with their caddies and teaching pros, and the atmosphere is relaxed. But, just as Sandra has said, do these women ever practise! They line the practice tees, hitting ball after ball into the stratosphere, and crowd a huge practice putting green. I spot Canadian pro Nancy Harvey, whom I met a few days ago at the Golf Ranch, where she was being photographed for Sandra's new magazine, *World of Women's Golf*. She's on the putting green holing putt after putt, up to thirty and forty feet away. Impressive.

I recognize lots of the women pros now, among them Alison Nicholas (prettier than she looks on TV and not as square, just *strong*-looking); Australian Karrie Webb, whose gorgeous eyes and dimple in the middle of her un-chin make up for her chinless TV profile; and the statuesque American Michelle McGann, looking magnificent in a solid black ensemble, long blonde ponytail trailing down her back, and wearing her trademark wide-brimmed hat. David points out Stefania Croce, a beauteous Italian player, who has more style without really trying than the entire field, including McGann with her modish but very studied look. Stefania is *not* studied, just indefinably chic. She's slightly built and wearing superbly cut white pants, a flashy belt, and the coolest pair of golf shoes I've ever laid eyes on. They're *turquoise*, and possess quintessentially Italian flair.

To my huge disappointment, Nancy Lopez is not here. She is, reportedly, burned out after her near win at the U.S. Open two weeks ago.

David and I tag along with a group of spectators being shepherded round the practice area by Québécoise pro Annie Chouinard (coach to LPGA pro Lorie Kane, who's from Prince Edward Island). Someone in our group comments that she has not spotted last year's du Maurier Classic champion, British golfer Laura

Davies, on the practice range. Oh, everyone knows that Laura *hates* practising, Annie grins. And the flamboyant, five-foot-ten, hefty Davies, who hits drive after drive more than 260 yards, is well known never to have taken a lesson, Annie adds. She is also known for her taste in machinery (she drives a Ferrari as well as a tractor), gambling, and a generally let-it-all-hang-out life.

Annie is full of fascinating information about the women's Tour. For example, the women's Tour sets aside a portion of the money it makes from pro-am tournaments (in which the pros play with amateurs, who pay handsomely for the privilege) for personal emergencies that can arise among fellow Tour members. Things such as a baby getting sick or an unexpected injury that leaves one of the pros suddenly short of cash. This, she says, is evidence of the camaraderie and *esprit de corps* within the LPGA Tour.

As for the ferocious practising we see all round us (by women already at the top of their sport): The practice sessions pros religiously follow during the two or three days before a major tournament are less about doing well in the tournament than they are about warming up, says Annie. Annie has often seen women do really well during practice and then bomb out during the tournament – and vice versa. In fact, some pros get spooked if they do really well during practice, thinking this means they'll crash for sure during the real thing.

As we stand behind the practice range, where more than twenty women pros are firing away, Annie has some interesting things to say about my old bugbear, alignment. Notice how these women are *always* precise about alignment when on the practice range, she says. If you hit a bad shot on target, it's just a bad shot, plain and simple. But if you hit a shot that's *not* on target – consistently – you have a swing fault you must work on. Hence the pros' careful attention to alignment when they're practising.

The pro-am tournament is on Wednesday. We arrive just in time to see Laura Davies tee off. She's in a mixed foursome that includes tournament organization heavyweights Jim Ritts, LPGA commissioner, and Don Brown, du Maurier chairman ("He's the man who writes the cheques," Sandra quips when I describe this scene to her), and Crawford Sandefur, an impeccably groomed woman who is a guest of Brown's. A sizeable crowd, including several press photographers, queues behind the ropes at the first tee. Davies is the draw: she's the defending champion, plus everyone loves a long hitter.

Laura is awesome to behold. She towers above her teammates, and she has shoulders from here to beyond there. She's wearing her "uniform": Bermuda shorts, matching hip-length vest, and a contrasting short-sleeved golf shirt. She arrived late last night, after squeezing in a charity tournament with Arnold Palmer in Seattle between the LPGA tournament in Ohio last week and this one. If she's jet-lagged, she doesn't show it. But rumours abound that she can't go on like this, burning the candle at both ends. She's known for her nerveless play; she doesn't even take practice swings before she tees off, just lets 'em fly. But yesterday the pressure of playing with a legend got to even Davies. "I just went to pieces," she said to reporters. "He [Palmer] was incredibly nice to me, and kept telling me not to worry, but I couldn't help myself. I four-putted a couple of times. Four-putted! I can't recall *ever* doing that." She grinned amiably. Nice to know she's human.

Laura tees off with her customary flair, exploding from her shoes, the ball screaming past the gallery and disappearing down the fairway. Next up, Jim Ritts, a trim, blond, preppy-looking chap, and Don Brown, short, lightly built, and dark-haired. I feel nervous on their behalfs. Hard to imagine having to tee off in front of a gallery that has just witnessed a force of nature like Laura Davies. Ritts and Brown survive the pressure; they both hit mighty drives. Next up, several yards down the fairway at the women's (front) tee, Crawford Sandefur tees off. She, too, drives well.

David and I set off with the little knot of spectators following Laura and her team. I fall into step just behind Ritts and Brown. Ritts is saying, "We got it in the air, Don, we got it in the air!" We arrive at the second tee. As Sandefur waits her turn to tee off, she says to her caddy, "My heart got an aerobic workout on that first tee!"

So all three of them *were* nervous. And in barely two weeks, *I* am going to be in their place. Sandra has signed me up in a corporate tournament at Lionhead Golf and Country Club in Brampton, Ontario, a course I do not know. Sandra reports that it is huge, far too long – and expensive – for me to venture out on a practice round before the actual tournament. Naturally this description does nothing to help my pre-tournament jitters! I've known about this tournament since the middle of May, but this is the first time it has seemed frighteningly real. Sandra and I, along with two experienced men players, will make up a foursome. The classy Sandefur, a portrait of cool and of chic, is my only role model for this experience. But will *my* nerves be able to stand it?

We follow the Davies foursome for a few more holes. Somewhere round the 4th hole, Brown crashes badly. He's hitting a fairway shot a few yards away from us. His ball flies sharply to the left, hits a small tree near the gallery area, and ricochets off it. He is not pleased. He retrieves his ball and hits another that skims the ground maybe fifty yards. Omigosh, that could have been me! David, too, notes this little scene with a sense of "There but for the grace of God go I."

Glorious but hot weather continues for the rest of the week. As David and I toil round the huge Glen Abbey course following the pros, who truly do move at Sandra's "Tour pace," I again rue the day I dismissed golf as no exercise. To my chagrin, David proves to have more stamina than I do. He seems to be able to stand in full sun longer without wilting, drink less water to keep going, and be less inclined to flag at the moment of decision about whether or not to "walk in" yet another player to her final hole.

On Thursday, Day One of the Classic, we watch a magnificent performance by Laura Davies on the par-5, 18th hole. First, she drives *way* past everyone else. Then, when the other players are "laying up" to avoid the water in front of the 18th green, she hangs back, waiting until they are all off the green to make a gutsy second shot over the pond.

All of this looks utterly nerveless to me. Laura never dawdles over a shot, and when she drives, she just lets her driver flit back and forth a few inches beside the ball in what looks like an extended stutter, before letting it fly. She's exhilarating to watch all right; everything she does looks so effortless and free. Laura's the Tiger Woods of this tournament, drawing the largest gallery by far.

But, as David astutely points out on this par-5, 18th hole, Laura's two competitors, Rosie Jones and Donna Andrews, both make the same score as Laura does – birdie 4s – without matching her showy long drives. They lay up short of the water, then chip onto the green and single putt. On her spectacular second shot, Laura clears the water beautifully, but the ball lands in a greenside bunker.

So, like the others, she is on the green only after three shots after all. Proof positive that strategy – and accuracy – can work just as well as long drives.

The four days we spend at the Classic really bring home to me David's nanomillimetre take on golf. To a raw beginner like me, the differences in these tournaments between the leaders and the followers, the winners and the could-have-beens, seem minute. They are *all* superb, including several pre-tournament favourites who do not make the cut this week, among them Karrie Webb, Alison Nicholas, Michelle McGann, and the brilliant Swedish crowd-pleaser Annika Sorenstam. And Laura Davies, despite all the hype, is not a contender. The Canadian star Dawn Coe-Jones – whom we see make a spectacular eagle on the 17th green on Thursday, a shot she describes as probably the best of her fifteen-year LPGA career (she chips into the hole, blind, from twenty yards away on a precipitous downhill lie behind a huge sand bunker) – misses the cut by one stroke. And the winner is forty-year-old American Colleen Walker, who has never won a major before and shoots an astonishing final round of 65.

After four days hanging out at Glen Abbey I think about what has impressed me the most watching these world-class women golfers. Well, their drives are, in a word, magnificent. But in general, once you've seen one you've seen 'em all. They're all high, beautifully curved, straight, long – not adjectives that would make the cut in a golf column written for people in the know. But for me, Raw Beginner, Lorie Kane's drive and Laura Davies' drive both look equally impressive, even though I *know* Laura's goes appreciably farther.

So, scratch the drives.

Next there are the putts. Well, it's fun watching the pros putt, because no matter how good a putter you are, you can still miss putts. Putting by definition is a matter of nuance, and when you add the monumental pressure under which the pros must perform, it's no wonder every major tournament is filled with near misses on the putting green. Upon which we, the watching rubes, can say smugly to ourselves, *we* might have made that.

So, scratch putting.

Then there are the sand shots. Yes, they're pretty impressive, especially when a player is in one of those really deep bunkers like the ones at Royal Troon, where photographs show only the head of the golfer above the lip. But of all the shots in golf, sand shots probably hold the least terror for me. Maybe because I've made some pretty impressive shots out of sand, including one at Oakville Executive's practice bunker a couple of weeks ago (as I boasted to Sandra, who was teaching a private lesson behind me at the time, I made a "hole in one" from a point in the bunker about twenty-five feet from the hole). One of the reasons sand doesn't scare me is because of Sandra's instruction to take a healthy chunk of sand with the shot. Taking a whole wallop of sand with the shot seems much easier than having to hit only that tiny, infernal ball. And the inhibitions I often feel about taking a divot on the fairway (and "messing up" the ground) leave me. I know I can't injure the sand, so I feel comfortable going for it.

So . . . I find great sand shots impressive but not awesome.

What does that leave? Chipping, pitching . . . and fairway shots. Well, scratch chipping and pitching, because there seem to be relatively few of these shots in pro tournaments. The pros tend to get onto the green in two or three long shots (one in the case of par 3s).

Which leaves the "approach shots" (the shot that aims for the green. On a par 5, this would be the third shot; on a par 4, the second; on a par 3, you aim for the green straight off). Pros' approach shots impress the hell out of me because they're so incredibly accurate. Pros know, with uncanny precision, both how far the shot will go and its exact direction. Both of which are galaxies beyond my capabilities at the moment.

After watching these experts do their thing on the golf course, the bottom line for me is awe. I am absolutely blown away by the consistently high standard of play. At no point (except during the pro-am!) do we see a flubbed drive or fairway shot. Never a whiff, never a topped ball, never a crazy miss going sharp right or left – nothing even close. I think back on my rounds with Sharon and Jan, and the nervous skittishness with which we monitor each other's shots – no matter where we're standing. But watching these pros, I feel utterly relaxed when they're about to hit the ball, no matter how close they are. Which brings me to another point: Golf is the only professional sport left in which you can scrutinize the pros literally within touching distance. Sure, watching a tournament on TV is more *efficient* (because the cameras can monitor every player in the tournament), but there's no way TV can compete with the thrilling immediacy of standing within two feet of a world-class player getting ready to tee off.

CHAPTER 15

DOWNWARD SPIRAL

Thanks to a week of dazzling *voyeuse* golf at Glen Abbey, I've barely picked up a club for seven days. And it's only two weeks now until the tournament at Lionhead. As my late Scottish father-in-law used to say, Time to get back to old clothes and porridge.

With any luck, some of the excellence I've seen over the past week will have improved my swing and my game by osmosis. Maybe I should try to go into a trance and imagine myself as Laura Davies. No, let's get a bit closer to home: how about the bouncy, always-smiling Lorie Kane, who ended the tournament with a respectable two strokes under par and clearly had a marvellous time doing it? Lorie's a terrific role model, very relaxed, obviously happy in her own skin. Not unlike Sandra, come to think of it.

Which brings me back to reality. I cannot let Sandra down at the tournament. Or, rather, I must not. Time to go into serious training for it.

I'm getting my woods this week. All two of them – a 5-wood and a 3-wood – which Sandra tells me is plenty for now. I wish I'd had them a month ago, but them's the breaks. Sandra's husband, John, has gone into business this year assembling customized golf clubs, and has the Canadian franchise for an American system called Every Shaft Precise (ESP). John analyses each customer's swing with a radar machine, then feeds the printout through ESP's highly specialized software system, which takes every single swing through an incredible thirty-thousand calculations. The result? Clubs with "every shaft precise" – meaning, essentially, that he calibrates the flex of your shaft ("the only part of your golf club that moves") to accommodate the speed and style of each person's unique golf swing. This apparently works even with a wildly inconsistent golf swing like mine.

I measure at the bottom of the scale – below it, actually. My 7-iron swing averages fifty-four miles per hour, and the slowest swing the computer reads is fifty-six miles per hour. Not to worry, John assures me. If they matched my speed and strength exactly, they'd have to give me a rubber band for a shaft! As it is, my shafts are very "whippy," which means they're easy on the body and create much less stress and vibration than the very stiff clubs of David's that I was using until I got my ESP irons about a month ago.

In her golf clinics, Sandra often talks about women inheriting their husband's golf clubs the way I did. Hubby, naturally enough, assumes wife shouldn't run out and buy her own clubs until she develops some expertise. Sandra agrees that new golfers shouldn't buy a set of expensive clubs immediately. But the problem with using hubby's old clubs "until she improves her swing" is that men's clubs invariably are much too heavy and stiff for women, *particularly* when women are just starting to play. Even Sandra, with the powerful swing she's been honing for forty-four years, recently discovered that she was using clubs that were far too stiff for her during her entire sixteen years on the Tour.

"Just *think* what I could have done with the right clubs!" she says. "In those days, you had to have much more raw talent to compensate for the inadequate clubs we were using. It's the same in every sport. Compare the marvellously light oversize tennis rackets that you can buy now with the ones on the market twenty years ago. The new equipment available to us just makes getting the job done a lot easier."

A STARTER GOLF BUDGET

GOLF CLUBS: A HALF-SET: $600

3-wood (to use for your tee shot)
5-wood (to use off the fairway)
pitching wedge or sand wedge (your choice)
8-iron or 9-iron (short iron)
6-iron or 7-iron (middle iron)
4-iron or 5-iron (long iron)
putter

Depending on whether you choose graphite or steel shafts and name-brand or generic clubs, a half-set can cost anywhere from $300 to $1,000. About $600 will buy you good equipment to start with.

GOLF BAG: $100 AND UP

It should be strong, lightweight, waterproof, and roomy.
• It should be strong enough to protect your shafts when travelling. If the bag is made of nylon, it should have metal rods inside for support.
• Whether you choose to carry your bag, buy or rent a pullcart, or golf using an electric cart, your bag should be lightweight enough for you to handle easily (you'll have to at least lift it out of your trunk and on and off your cart).
• Make sure the bag comes with a detachable head cover in case of rain and for travelling.
• Make sure your golf bag has at least three roomy pockets. A pocket for small items (golf balls, tees, pencils, markers, divot repairer); a pocket for extra clothing (rain jacket, sweater, cap, or visor); a pocket for a drink and energy snack.
• If your clubs have graphite shafts, the bag should have soft material around the inside edge of the bag. Avoid plastic tubes to keep your clubs apart; they're more of a hindrance than a help and do not allow your grips to dry.

GOLF EQUIPMENT

- Golf balls (about six, made of surlyn or a blend) $10
- Package of tees plus ball repairer $1.50
- A few small coins for markers
- Golf towel $10
- Golf shoes $100
- Golf glove $15
- Headcovers for your clubs $30
- Golf ball retriever $20

GOLF CLOTHING

You can spend as much or as little as you like on golf clothing. Begin with a pair of Bermuda shorts, a cotton shirt with a collar and sleeves, a cap or visor, a vest or sweater, and a waterproof jacket.

OTHER ITEMS TO CARRY IN YOUR GOLF BAG

- Sunscreen
- Band-Aids
- Plastic bottle of water, energy snack (nuts, chocolate bar, apple)

I've been using my new irons for about a month now and I love them (I have four – a 4-, 6-, and 8-iron, and a pitching wedge). They have oversize generic clubheads and true-temper release-steel shafts. Steel is less expensive than graphite, and the generic clubheads, of course, are less expensive than brand-name models. So, although I've paid a bit more for my custom-made clubs, the total price is not much more than they would have cost if I'd bought them "off the rack."

Today I drive to the Golf Ranch to pick up my two new woods, which John has just finished assembling. They're graphite. I'm very excited.

"Now let's see where I've put them," John says. "Oh yes. Here they are." He pulls two woods off a shelf in his tiny workshop. The heads are encased in heavy plastic. "We got you champagne. That's all that was available." Champagne? Does he mean top of the line? I'm mystified. "Champagne," John repeats. He shows me the shaft. "The colour."

Oh! I'm so glad that was all that was available. They're beautiful. The subtle colour is like a wedding dress trying not to look white. I cut the heads free from their protective wraps, uncovering oversize heads with a heft that look as if they'll have no trouble finding the ball. John holds my new 5-wood by both ends, flexing the shaft. Yes, I can see that it's wonderfully flexible. Light, too, I discover as I pick it up. I'm thrilled and excited, anxious to try them out.

To the practice range! I assemble my full arsenal of clubs: pitching wedge, 4-, 6-, 8-irons, and, the *pièces de résistance*, my two beautiful new woods. I do everything by the book. I start with warm-up stretching exercises. Then move on to my pitching wedge. Then my 8-, my 6-, my 4-iron . . . and my 5-wood.

But something is going terribly, terribly wrong. *I can't get the ball off the ground.* I am alone on the practice range. John is in his workshop. He has a full, untrammelled view of my practice station. He comes to my rescue.

"You're pulling up," he says. "You're trying to see where the ball has gone instead of keeping your head down for a split second after impact." Good point. I hit the ball again. It skids along the ground.

"Now look at that left arm," John says. "It's breaking down on you. You're pulling in . . . like this." He shows me what I'm doing. "You know what happens if you do that? It means you're *sure* to top the ball."

Unhuh. I try again. The ball skids along the ground.

"Now don't be doing this." John is really trying hard to help me now. "What you're doing, you see, is baseball! You're swinging the club like a baseball bat," John enlarges. "Parallel to the ground, not pointing one shoulder towards the ball on the backswing and the other shoulder towards the ball on the follow-through."

I lean towards the ball. Or, rather, I try to. All of a sudden my shoulders feel horribly stiff.

The ball skids along the ground.

It's noon. The sun is nailing me to the ground. I take a swig of water and try to remember what John has told me. Um. . . . baseball. Something about baseball.

And my left arm . . . I'm pulling it in. And my head. Yes, my head. It's looking up. Don't look up.

I take another swing at the ball. It skids along the ground.

"You know what your problem is?" John's face lights up. He's got the answer, I'm sure of it. "It's paralysis by analysis!" he says. "What you're doing is stopping on your backswing – thinking too much about what you're about to do – and then, after you pause – and you pause *far* too long! – your swing gets choppy. Bad timing. No rhythm."

I remember my resolution to put myself into a trance. Lorie Kane was my model. I try to visualize Lorie's happy, smiling face.

I hit the ball. It skids along the ground.

"You know what, Loral?" John says. From the look on his face, I know he has it this time. "It's alignment. Your problem is alignment." He shows me an arrow on the clubhead of my new 5-wood. "Now, all you do is align this arrow towards something about six inches in front of your clubhead – something that's in line with the target."

I hit the ball. It skids along the ground.

"Loral, I've got it." From John's tone I just know we've wrestled this thing to the ground. "It's your stance. You're *sitting down*! You're not bending from your waist – like so – sticking your tush out. And look at your *arms*!" I try to get a glom on my arms. "What it is, is they're not hanging comfortably by your sides. They're out here. See?" He shows me where my arms are. He's right. They're out here. Not hanging comfortably. "And while you're at it," John adds, "why don't you adjust those shoulders so that your left shoulder is higher than your right one?"

Yes, of course.

I look at my watch. I've been here almost two hours. I gather up my clubs.

"I'm going home to lick my wounds." I look down at the ground. I know that if I look up I'm going to burst into tears.

"Bet you're wondering why you ever decided to take up this game," John says gently. I nod my head, trying not to snuffle.

I flee to the safety of the car, put my foot on the gas pedal, and accelerate onto Highway 10. Heading south, homeward bound. I wipe my eyes under my glasses. Don't fog up, you dumb suckers! My mind is a mess. All those lessons . . . two weeks until the tournament . . . my beautiful new woods . . . the pro-am tournament. Was it only five days ago? *And every single tee-off I saw was a stunning sky-high shot.* Not one person flubbed.

SO WHAT'S WRONG WITH ME? Am I a total, irredeemable klutz?

Ten days until the tournament now, and David is taking pity on me. He suggests we go together to a driving range where I can practise with my new woods. My "golf station" in the backyard simply doesn't cut it with woods, he says. "The whole idea of using woods is to let it all hang out, let it rip. You can't get the feel by banging away at pine cones in the backyard."

We drive to a practice range I've recently discovered north of the city called Larkin Farms. It's run out of an old family barn, tastefully decorated with red geraniums in window boxes. The range is peaceful and lovely, stretching into gently rolling farmers' fields in the distance.

We get there on a Saturday morning ahead of the heat and the crowds. I am filled with early-morning hope. I work my way through Sandra's practice routine – start with stretching exercises, then on to my pitching wedge, short irons, long irons, woods. Alas, my problems are still with me. I cannot seem to get balls off the ground.

David is all sympathy. He suggests I go back to a half-swing, at least on my backswing, since I seem to have lost control of it: my clubhead falls back at a crazed angle and wraps itself behind my head. I scroll back hazily to Sharon and me at that first clinic with Sandra so long ago. Sharon was so grateful for Sandra's instruction about the half-swing, saying it helped her get back in control of her full swing. And earlier this morning on Radio 640's weekly golf show (the one Sandra has hosted a few times this summer), I heard a similar tip from pro Paul Wilson. He advised swinging the club "waist-high. Everyone can relate to 'waist-high.' If you concentrate on this, you'll probably swing it much higher, but you're also much more likely to keep the club under control."

I try this and, sure enough, I do swing the club higher than waist-high, but I also no longer wrap my clubhead round the back of my neck. I start hitting the ball off the ground with my 4-iron, about eighty yards.

And eventually I manage to hit a few balls off the ground with my 5-wood. I grip down on the shaft a lot: the length throws me. I still like the way they feel. They feel as if it should be a cinch to hit the ball with them, because they're so light and have those hefty big heads.

A week now until the tournament. I go back to Larkin Farms this morning, by myself. And I do *terribly*. I've hit a wall for sure this time. I just want this tournament to be over with. I want to get back to a sane life.

The whole rigmarole is really getting to me. For starters, I'm sick to death of the driving. I've gone to such lengths to find practice ranges within a reasonable distance. But my calculations just don't work in summer city traffic! I estimate forty minutes to drive to the practice range, and plan to get away early and be home by lunchtime. Well, forget that. It takes me almost an hour and a half to get to the range after battling construction and heavy traffic, plus a couple of unavoidable pit stops for gas and a bank machine.

Finally I have my bucket of balls and I'm ready to go. It's a perfect day, not hot, and I'm alone on the range. I go through my regular practice routine, adding another wrinkle to help keep myself focused: I decide I'll progress from one iron to the next as soon as I've hit five good shots with each one.

It takes me a full hour, plus a jumbo bucket of balls, to get through twenty decent shots. It is a painful hour. I top the ball, bump-and-run it, you name it. I feel stiff. I try to turn my left shoulder towards the ball the way John reminded me to do and, as soon as I attempt this, my left arm bends in two. I remember Dana's "chicken wings" on that long-ago first round at Flemingdon. I concentrate on keeping my left arm straight, and when that doesn't work I tell myself to concentrate on "just clipping the tee." This is one of *Little Red Book* author Harvey Penick's wise tips for students who can't get the ball off the ground. It works wonders for Harvey's students. And on me? No effect, zip.

And I haven't yet started on my woods! I buy another bucket of balls. The owner, a sympathetic man, suggests I move to the artificial tee-off pads with rubber tees. I was avoiding them, thinking they'd make things unrealistically easy. But now I welcome easy. At least *one* chore is eliminated: jamming the damned tee into the earth, which is hard and dry after weeks of sunny weather.

ANOTHER ASIDE FROM SANDRA (AS PROMISED)

Remember Loral's throwaway line, "When am I going to have a really bad day?" – and my rejoinder, "This will come back to haunt her." I watch hundreds of my students go through the same roller coaster of emotions that Loral is experiencing. It's perfectly natural and is to be expected. She wouldn't believe me if I said this to her now, but Loral *will* get through this.

Like a mantra, I remind myself: (1) keep left arm straight on the backswing; (2) shift weight first to right foot, then to left; (3) tilt shoulder towards ball; (4) follow through to face target; (5) keep head down, down, down; (6) hit *down* on ball; (7) keep backswing *smooth*; (8) don't pause too long on backswing; (9) don't rush it, either; (10) use hips and legs, not just arms; (11) bend at waist; keep back straight; DON'T SIT.

And (12) – stop thinking so much!

By the time I start on my woods, I'm mentally and emotionally exhausted. Wearily, I force myself to use the entire shaft. It's the length, supposedly, that gives woods extra distance. I manage this feat without gouging the Astroturf with the clubhead, but it makes no difference to the distance. In desperation, I switch back to my 4-iron, the club I've been using up until now to tee off with, a club I thought I felt comfortable with. And now *it* feels heavy and clumsy. I hit just as badly with it, maybe worse.

CHAPTER 16

ROCK BOTTOM

Three days until the tournament. I'm sitting on our front veranda, one of my favourite places in the whole world, on a beautiful August morning. The cicadas are buzzing, the air is warm, a light breeze flutters over the big wicker chair I'm curled up in. And I'm hung over. Devoid of energy and motivation. Depressed. Filled with self-loathing. I cannot think of anything I would less rather do than swing a golf club, ever again. Last spring when Sandra and I discussed this "great" idea – me, the middle-aged, non-athletic, blah, blah, blah woman taking up golf *intensely* over the summer – it all seemed such a lark. Not golf particularly, but the whole endeavour. Learning it all from ground zero, being Sandra's protegée . . . It was going to be such fun.

And now. It's the dog days of summer. I'm flat out of energy. I'm sick of that four-letter word: G O L F. I just want this all to be over.

Things have been imploding for . . . how long? It's all a jumble in my mind. I think I started going downhill in earnest the day I picked up my woods at the Golf Ranch. When was that, two weeks ago maybe? And John was so helpful, pointing out at least ten things wrong with my swing. As I left I said, "I'm going home to lick my wounds." I remember he looked surprised – I guess he hadn't realized how discouraged I was – and said something consoling. Which I didn't listen to. Instead, I drove home, playing the tape over and over inside my head: all my errors, all my swing faults. By the time I got home I was feeling very, very sorry for myself.

I recently read about a golf pro who takes the standard golf philosophy of playing the game one shot at a time an extra notch: when he hits a bad shot or, indeed, when he plays an entire bad round (bad, by *his* standards), he does not acknowledge it in any way. Not now, not ever. He just goes forward, never admitting it ever happened, never saying anything negative, never exhibiting any anger or emotion. He just calmly goes on to the next stroke, and concentrates on that.

When I first read this story, I thought this behaviour sounded very unhealthy. Obviously, this person was repressing what had happened, bottling it up. He was in denial. But the behaviour worked! It allowed him to concentrate totally on each shot as it came, erasing past and future failures and triumphs, freeing him up to go on, unencumbered.

The pro in question is American PGA pro Tom Watson, David says, winner of eight majors and one of his heroes. As I try now to analyse why my swing is getting worse and worse no matter how much I practise, I wonder if perhaps the whole cycle started with my abject admission to John about how discouraged I felt. It got imprinted on my brain and became a self-fulfilling prophecy.

Since then, every time I've practised I've done terribly. And the last time, I did worse with my "trusty" irons than with my untested woods! This leaves me with a dilemma for the tournament: whether to use my woods and chance it, knowing it's entirely hit and miss, or go back to my irons when I tee off and risk looking *really* stupid. People will watch and say, "Oh, she can't use woods yet – understandable; she's just a beginner. So she'll use her irons . . . oops! She can't even hit with her irons!"

Yesterday I played Flemingdon with Sharon and Jan. My twelfth round of the summer, an even dozen. And I played what is without question my worst round of golf ever. The worst part about it was how *nice* everyone was about it. Jan and Sharon outdid themselves with kindnesses. They assiduously tried to help. All to no avail. I just topped the ball over and over again.

My putting was okay, and I forced myself to take more time with it, trying to buck up my spirits. But I swear it's impossible to enjoy golf if only your short game is working! I defy *anyone* to disagree with this. It just doesn't help.

I talked to Sandra last night. She had to host Tim O'Connor's "Bell Canada Golf Hour" on Radio 640 this morning, so she was distracted. But when I told her my game had gone to ratshit, and that I'd played today and simply couldn't hit the ball, and that I'd been to a few driving ranges, and . . . she broke in and said, "Don't overtrain."

Don't overtrain. I know I must take this to heart. Especially coming from a pro. God knows, she's been there. When I think about the number of tournaments – tournaments that really matter – that *she's* played! Overtraining must be like cramming for an exam the night before, instead of doing your homework, studying all year long, and then being confident you've covered the ground.

What Sandra didn't realize, of course, is that I'm *not* overtraining. Sure, I've been practising. But *I just cannot hit the ball any more.*

My friend Linda, a painter who spends long hours alone in front of her canvases, has given me excellent advice. Excellent, that is, if the world were unfolding as it should be right now after my Summer of Golf. Her advice assumed I'd been practising all summer and progressing slowly but surely, and now the Big Test is coming. In any endeavour, she said, there are times when, no matter how highly trained you are, you just don't get it together. It happens. There's nothing you can do about it if it's not going to be great. The one thing you can do is be calm within yourself.

Yes, Linda. Excellent advice. Be calm within myself. But, you see, I can't hit the ball any more!

David has been very sympathetic. He filled me with wine last night and fired away with prognostications. Such as: "Julie Inkster was thinking exactly the same thing about herself as you are now, on the 18th hole of the last day of the du Maurier Classic. She'd been close to the lead for the entire tournament and then, with her last two *disastrous* shots – shots no professional golfer should ever make, one into a tree and the next into the water – she lost the tournament." Then he adds his mantra: "You can hit one shot off the tee that soars straight, 150 yards. And then, the next shot you hit veers right, hits the ground, whatever. And it's all because you changed one tiny little thing . . . like the angle of your clubface. It's the most maddening of games. A game of nanomillimetres." And if he says that one more time, I think I'll wrap my lovely 5-wood around his neck.

As Sandra hung up, she said, "Come to the Ranch over the weekend if you feel like it. I'll be there."

It's my only hope. Tomorrow, the Golf Ranch for one last practice session with Sandra.

David comes with me this morning to the Golf Ranch for my final tune-up. When we arrive, Sandra is getting ready to teach a clinic. David says hello, then retreats to the commercial side of the range with a bucket of balls.

"Hey, Loral, I really like your hair!" Sandra says. I got my hair cut quite short this week. "Did you do that just for the tournament? You're starting to look like a golfer. Partly the hair – easy to care for *and* it makes you look younger – but I like your golf shorts and your golf shoes, too."

Sandra looks tired. She's been here since 8:15 this morning, she says. Yesterday she hosted the golf show from 7 to 8 A.M., then taught the entire day afterwards.

I fill a bucket of balls and set myself up adjacent to Sandra's teaching area, far enough away to keep out of the way. The women are arriving now; it's a young, chic-looking group. As I do my warm-up exercises, I hear Sandra's voice as she starts the clinic. You'd never guess she was exhausted. It's her trademark bright chirp, energy flowing. No doubt about it, Sandra puts out. She gives teaching her all. *Nobody* gets short-changed.

Except me. I spend almost two hours practising, and Sandra barely gives me a single tip. Except: "Looks good, but the backswing is too short." To which I retort, "That's what I'm *trying* to do, because I've lost control of the full backswing." She turns back to the women in her clinic. "Sound familiar?" she grins.

The one consolation in my entire practice session: I'm consistent. I consistently top the ball. Badly.

Yeah. Bad joke.

I've been hacking away for more than an hour. David comes over, having emptied his bucket of balls, and tells me he has no idea why I'm topping the ball. "You'll have to get some input from Sandra." But Sandra is busy. I continue to try to hit balls alone.

John arrives. David comes back, having finished a session on the putting green now. The two of them start taking an inordinate interest in my progress. *All I want is to be left alone!* I want to scream. They both scrutinize me. I feel like the most over-analysed golfer since the beginning of time.

John starts to talk and he makes sense, dammit. I'm pulling up. I'm pulling my arms in, instead of letting them swing. I'm locking my knees as I swing through, instead of keeping them relaxed. I'm (once again) holding my hands too far from my body.

"Don't 'wuss' the ball," John says. "Give it some muscle!" *Wuss*. The three of us discuss the word. We agree it's a good one. How should we spell it? "Wuss" with two s's, we decide, because it rhymes with "puss."

I continue to hack away. And then, out of the blue, I suddenly start hitting the

---

SANDRA'S TEACHING TIP

DON'T LEAVE YOUR BEST SHOTS ON THE PRACTICE TEE

Before you go out for a round of golf, you should hit a few balls on the practice tee to loosen up. But don't overdo it. Save your energy for the golf course. If you're a beginner, hitting twenty to twenty-five balls is enough to warm up. If you hit any more than that, you'll find you've left your best shots on the practice range, and by the 12th hole or so, you'll be exhausted.

When you practise, start with your shortest, easiest club, probably your 9-iron. Hit two or three shots with it, then go on to your 7-iron and your 5-iron. Then finish off with your 5-wood and your 3-wood or driver.

Go to the practice putting green and take a few putts to get a feel for the speed of the green. Now you're ready to go to the first tee.

ball off the ground. After an hour and a half. With my 5-wood. At this moment, only David is here. What have I done differently? I ask. He has no idea.

"Just do whatever you just did, again," he says. I hit the ball again. It soars up into the air. I hit it again. Up it goes. And again. "I think she's back," David says to John, who has just walked out of his workshop.

"Don't leave all your good shots here!" Sandra yells from inside her office.

I wish.

And now, again ensconced in my wicker chair on our front veranda on a hot Sunday evening, I feel resigned to Tuesday's tournament. Whatever happens will happen. Sandra believes in fate (so long as you prepare and train and you're focused, etc., etc.). My biggest worry is this: I don't want to embarrass Sandra. Have I said this before? Yes, I know I have. But she's been so generous with her time and expertise – even if she hasn't given me one-on-one hand-holding! *All* that instruction . . . I don't want to let her down.

David thinks I should go out to a driving range tomorrow and try to get some confidence with my woods. I don't agree. I think I should be quiet the day before the tournament. No cramming! As Linda said, Be calm within yourself.

NIGHT BEFORE TOURNAMENT: SANDRA PREDICTS . . . AND REMEMBERS

Loral called me a couple of nights ago. She's panicked. She can't hit the golf ball! she says. And she's worried about the tournament. I don't think she realizes how easy the scramble format is, even though her friends have reassured her. (We'll play in a foursome and follow the best ball hit on every shot. Our team has to use only two of Loral's drives.) But she wants to do better. And that's to be expected.

So I tell her to come to my practice range and loosen up, get her confidence back. David comes with her and helps her, because I'm busy teaching. Her problem was she'd gotten stiff in the knees: she wasn't flexing them. That's the kind of thing that happens when you're trying too hard. You get tight.

Anyway, she fixed it and she's back. She's more relaxed, and she's hitting the golf ball. I'm not worried about her at all tomorrow. Not that she won't be nervous! Of course she'll be nervous. She'll probably have a hard time sleeping tonight. And maybe she won't be able to eat tomorrow morning. But she's going to do it. She's going to play in the tournament, and she's going to get through it. And then she'll be free. That's the way it goes with tournaments. Once you make that first step into one, once you get over that hurdle, then you're free and clear after that.

We're playing at Lionhead Golf and Country Club in Brampton, Ontario – a very large, long . . . *huge* golf course. Bigger, probably, than any golf course Loral has ever seen. This tournament is for charity and for fun, and I don't really care what we shoot. But, in fact, I *know* we're going to do well, because we have two very good golfers in our foursome. Rob owns a golf store and he's a former club champion. And Harold owns a small public golf course and has been surrounded all his life by women who play golf. Both Rob and Harold know Loral is a new golfer. They've seen it all before; they certainly won't mind. And *I* certainly won't mind, no matter what Loral does! I've played in more tournaments than I can count – pro-ams, charity, corporate, you name it. And I've seen just about everything. I've played with politicians and businesspeople and dozens of film stars, and I've played with people who've never picked up a golf club before.

During my days on the LPGA Tour I was not nervous, exactly, before a tournament. It would more accurately be described as a keyed-up state. Of course, those tournaments involved my livelihood, my career. On the final day in a tournament, on the Sundays I was in contention, I really had to pace myself. I'd get up about three hours before tee-off and go through my morning routine slowly, make sure I took my time getting dressed, eating breakfast, driving to the golf course, and going through my practice routine on the driving range. For me, it was very important to keep everything slow. Not to rush, or my swing tempo would be fast. That was what I had to work on: not getting too fast in my swing.

I have lots of pre-tournament memories. But my most vivid one by far is from 1979, during the LPGA Colgate Dinah Shore Classic, which we were playing in Rancho Mirage near Palm Springs, California. I was defending the title I'd won in 1978. Defending a championship is very, very difficult. But I felt completely in control before, and all through, that tournament.

I was in competition with Nancy Lopez. At the turn, after nine holes, Nancy had me by two shots. And that didn't seem to bother me. I just knew, at that point, that the tournament had really started. I birdied the 10th, 11th, and 12th holes. Nancy was in front of me and the leaderboard was slow in recording my score, so the gallery was still thinking Nancy was leading. But I knew we were at least even by now. The caddies always know what's really happening, and between them and the roar of the crowd, you know where you stand. We got to the 16th hole and I made a twenty-foot putt for birdie. This was very dramatic because Nancy had bogeyed the 17th. Then I knew for sure I had a two-shot lead with two holes to play. I parred 17. Then Nancy birdied the 18th and I parred it . . . and I won by one stroke!

Like I said, I really felt in control that day. I just kept plodding along, making things happen. That's what you have to do to win tournaments: stay in control, stay focused on what you have to do to get it done, not on what everybody else is doing. Because you can't control what anybody else is doing; you can only control yourself (hopefully!).

And that's what Loral has to think of, on a much smaller scale. She doesn't have to think about how far I'm going to hit the ball or how far Rob's going to hit it or what Harold's going to do in this foursome. She has to think about Loral and about what Loral has learned in these past three months and what Loral is going to do.

She's just got to stand up there and do the things that she has learned. And she's been practising; I know she's been practising. I've really resisted going out of my way to help her because I wanted her to do this for herself. And there are no shortcuts. Learning to play golf is not easy. You have to be dedicated and you have to have discipline. And Loral has both of those. I know she's been out to play with her young nephew, and she's done things she never would have done in the past. Things she would never think she could have done in the past. But staying focused, and having this discipline, has changed her. She's a different personality. She's a lot more confident in herself (even though she's just a little bit nervous about this pro-am). But come Tuesday night she'll be at the post-tournament dinner, and she'll be laughing and she'll be so pleased that she did it. That she's one of us, that she's a golfer! She made it. And she didn't do it for David, she didn't do it for me, she didn't do it for her friends – she did it for herself, for Loral. She's been very determined, and she's worked very hard. And yes, she has a long way to go. But boy, she's well down that road.

I'm a few years younger than Loral, but we both grew up in the 1940s and 1950s and we remember the same heroes. Our icons were Barbara Ann Scott, Marilyn Bell, Marlene Stewart-Streit – women who were really something, admired because they had accomplished wonderful feats. Since my family loved sports, my heroes were sports heroes, and when I took up golf, my heroes were golfers. Marilynn Smith was my idol when I was a little girl, and when Kathy Whitworth started to win big, she became my hero. I met her when I was fourteen, and I was in complete awe of her.

But the day I turned pro and found myself on the first tee, I had no idols or heroes. We were on a level playing field now. I still respected these women, but there was no more awe. I wouldn't have been able to compete with them if I'd continued to put them on pedestals.

I'm not saying that Loral has ever been in awe of me, or that I've ever been her hero. But she certainly was intimidated by me at first, especially when she saw me hit the ball and she could barely swing her club. I've noticed a gradual, subtle change in her attitude towards me as her game has improved. She's much freer with me, and even makes jokes at my expense now and again. The biggest change, though, is in her attitude towards herself. As her confidence in her golf skills has grown, her attitude towards me, and everything connected with golf, has changed. She no longer hangs on my every word without questioning anything. There are times when she actually takes me to task on some golf matter, even something fairly technical! Sometimes I wonder what I have created.

I know David is wondering these days what he's gotten himself into . . .

Anyway, tomorrow will tell its own tale. How will Loral deal with the pressure? She certainly doesn't thrive on it the way I do. She's not a high-energy, let's-get-going kind of person like me. Not that I haven't had my own problems with pressure. I won nine LPGA tournaments and I came second in twenty — and if I could rewrite my own life, of course I'd turn those figures around.

Actually, it took me many years to understand myself mentally on the golf course. When you're on the Tour and you're out there at least four hours a day and you're down to the last nine holes and you're in a position to win, funny things go on. There's a lot of time to think in golf, time for negative thoughts as well as positive ones. There's adrenalin, of course, but there are also a lot more variables. What you have to go through to learn how to win can't be summed up in a paragraph or two.

To get back to tomorrow: well, it would be silly to claim the stakes are in the same league for me this time, but for Loral . . . For Loral it's not going to get any more exciting than this. I know this tournament is weighing heavily on her mind and that's okay, because she should take it seriously. But she's ready — even if she doesn't think she is.

And this tournament is just the beginning for Loral. Because this game is going to change her life. That's what I love about my life now, post-Tour, as teacher-mentor to new golfers. I can change people's lives forever. Now that's powerful. That's the magic of golf.

PART III: FROM FIRST SWING TO TOURNAMENT IN A SINGLE SEASON

CHAPTER 17

THE TOURNAMENT

I don't lose my appetite the day before the tournament, as Sandra predicted. But I'm in a state of nervous alert all day, unable to do anything except clearing-up and organizing tasks. I tidy my office, do some filing, assemble my golf equipment and wardrobe. I put a bottle of water in the fridge; I'll be sure, for once, to have *cold* water. I try on my outfit to be certain everything does up, zippers work, it all fits. I set out a new tube of suntan lotion, make sure I have half a dozen tees handy in my shorts pocket, choose a few respectable-looking balls (remembering John and Sandra's disdain for a crummy range ball I used during one of our rounds at Oakville), put coins in my pocket to mark the ball on the green. I decide not to clean my clubs: I like them battle-weary, grass marks in all the wrong places (toe, heel, sole), proving I consistently miss the sweet spot. I also decide against polishing my golf shoes: they're clean enough, and I'll probably just make a mess of them, smudging white polish over the suede saddle-shoe middles. I worry about my hair. My new short hairdo is barely a week old and hasn't quite settled in yet. It's too dry after washing; little wispy ends get away on me. Should I use gel? Or mousse? Nothing really seems to work and I resign myself to a bad-hair day. I worry about make-up: if I wear next to none I look totally washed out; if I slather it on it's likely to run when I sweat. I decide on a light coat and resolve to keep checking for mascara blotch.

Just before dinner, I practise in the backyard at my golf station – even taking some swings with my 5-wood. I put lots of energy into this practice session, determined not to wuss the "ball." I hit maybe half a dozen impressive-looking "balls" (as impressive as pine cones travelling fifteen yards can be). By the time I finish, I feel reasonably confident: I think I've loosened up.

I work on a picture in my mind's eye of Tiger Woods gracefully hitting the ball, coming down through it before following through. My mental image of this is very clear, and I hope that playing and replaying this tape through my mind will prevent me from lifting my head too soon and topping the ball. I try to sleep on it.

I'm in bed by 11 P.M. and sleep fitfully, never fully relaxing, half waking often. I get up at 7 A.M., do half an hour of yoga in the living room ("Be calm within yourself"), dress, eat breakfast, then take a few practice swings at my golf station. I feel reasonably confident. I'm *very* wired. I'm ready for whatever comes now, ready for fate to take charge. I just want to get on with it.

Sandra has left a telephone message that I've replayed several times, in which she says that I've done my homework, that I'm as prepared as I ever will be, and that I'll be fine. "You just have to trust me on this," she says, as she signs off. I do.

David (pictured on page 182) is being marvellously supportive. He's even offered to be my caddy! But carts are obligatory at Lionhead, so he's just going to tag along with our foursome and watch.

We leave home at 10:20 A.M. Lionhead is west and north of us on Mississauga Road, a route I haven't checked out in my quest for golf facilities within reasonable driving distances. We pass several large practice ranges and golf courses as we approach Lionhead. I'm amazed at the number of golf facilities ringing the city.

A large sign outside Lionhead heralds it as Canada's finest public golf facility. The entrance, parking area, and clubhouse are all huge. The feel of the place to my untrained eye is not unlike Glen Abbey, although I fear this may be heresy. They're both commodious, well-tended, expensively maintained golf courses – the difference being that Glen Abbey is built to challenge expert players in major tournaments and provide easy viewing by large galleries, and Lionhead, which includes not one but two eighteen-hole courses, is built for easy riding for corporate outings. Both have large dining areas and meeting rooms for big tournaments and business groups. Neither is my kind of

golf facility. My kind of clubhouse is small, cosy, and friendly; my kind of course is natural, not overly manicured, walker friendly.

We arrive just before 11 A.M. Tee-off time is not until 12:45 P.M., but the place is already packed. Ninety per cent of the people I see are middle-aged men, my old stereotype of The Golfer. The practice tee is crowded. The clubhouse is abuzz. Sandra spots us in the crowd and trots over at a fast clip to greet us. She looks terrific: skin aglow but no obvious make-up, a "together" outfit – dark plaid shorts, cream-coloured vest, navy shirt, white visor, blue-and-white golf shoes. She's bursting with energy and high spirits. Immediately, I feel welcome, protected, more confident. "Here, let me show you how you get a locker to put these things away," she says. She leads me into the ladies' locker room. And lo and behold, there's a locker in front of us, key in door, *with my name on it* – not a mere sticker, a permanent-looking metal plaque. It's misspelled, but there's no doubt that it's me they're after! So this is what corporate golf outings provide: one-day status made to look permanent. I'm truly stunned.

Sandra leads me out to our golf cart. This, too, has our names on it. It's sitting in the midst of a sea of little vehicles in a long, double-breasted line. Four bottles of mineral water are neatly lined up in racks in front of our seats (after all that trouble I took to chill my bottle of tap water). Sandra shows me how to properly strap my golf bag in the back. Everything tickety-boo and in place.

"Now we're going to the practice range," Sandra says authoritatively. "We just take one or two clubs with us, not our whole bag." I obediently remove my 6-iron

and my dreaded 5-wood. We march up to the tee, and I start flailing away. Topping the ball, of course. Sandra stands behind me and assesses the problem. Then she fixes several things, most importantly my grip. Unbeknownst to me, it's slipped round the handle into a "weak" position. I hope this has been my undiscovered problem and that I will hit just fine again. And I *do* hit a couple of good balls, and with my 5-wood yet. Already I feel much better. Sandra has a wonderful booster effect: helping, fixing, and goosing confidence all at the same time. "You want to stop there?" she asks, after I fire off a decent shot. I do. She marches me down the hill, back to our cart. Splendidly embossed Lionhead tags now hang on our golf bags, our names printed on them in solid black letters. *Gosh.*

I'm all fired up now, ready to go. But that's not how it's done. First, lunch, which is basic corporate-picnic fare: buffet service on a huge covered veranda – coleslaw, potato salad, sliced tomatoes, tossed salad, choice of hamburger or grilled chicken burger. And a sea of men milling about, schmoozing. "There are only sixteen of *us*," Sandra whispers. Sixteen women and 280 men.

Tee-off time at last. The scene is combination Disneyland and George Orwell's *Nineteen Eighty-Four.* A booming loudspeaker instructs us to take our positions. Everyone sits two-by-two in a numbered golf cart, obediently at the ready. A starter pistol fires, and off we go, a stately procession of shiny green toys on a paved path curving down a hill. I look back and see the hundred or so cute little electric carts proceeding in pairs, bulging golf bags standing erect behind, as if on guard. A mini-train at a zoo, a giant Lego set . . . ? Strange and bizarre. I scratch my head. Can this be me?

But questions of self and identity blur in my mind as I try to focus on tee-off. My only image of teeing off at a tournament is the pro-am at the LPGA du Maurier Classic: yellow ropes to keep the gallery at bay; a little tent to disappear into and freshen up in before emerging into the glare of the noontime sun and

the expectant spectators; stylishly uni-
formed marshals with their arms raised to
keep the gaping gallery hushed as each
player tees off.

Sandra is driving; I'm in the passenger
seat; David stands behind with the golf
bags. In tandem with us, in another cart,
are our teammates, Rob and Harold, whom
I've just met. We stop at the 3rd tee. I look
back. Only half a dozen carts are behind us
now; the path must have forked some-
where. We climb out. Sandra says, "Well, want to go ahead, Loral?"

*Sandra and me
with Harold
(left) and Rob.*

I stumble up to the teeing ground with my 5-wood, trying to blank out the
filled carts I know are sitting patiently behind. I have no swing thought. *Just do it!*
I hiss to myself. I can't see the flag, only what looks like a ravine ahead, a distance
I might be able to hit to on my best days. I take a deep breath, blank out the
people behind, and Just Do It.

And, to my amazement, the ball flies. In the air. Slightly leftward (a pull?). No
matter. A decent distance, with a decent arc. I am utterly dumbfounded, utterly
relieved. I wobble off the teeing area and weave back to the cart, unaware of my
teammates, of the protocol of watching respectfully while *they* tee off.

I've done it.

The ball, one I chose so carefully yesterday, is lost in woods I haven't even seen
until now, front and left of the ravine. Immaterial. There are more balls in this
world. In fact, Sandra already has given me a fistful of balls left in the cart for us.
Something tells me we're not at Flemingdon any more, Loral. This is an expan-
sive country called corporation golf, the Golfland of Oz. For my second ball of
the tournament, I choose one with Lionhead's crest on it.

Rob, Harold, and Sandra tee off. David walks ahead to the next tee, and the
four of us whizz off behind him in our trusty little carts. My confidence is up. I've
passed the 1st tee. Let the tournament begin.

What happens next? Nothing. Precisely nothing. From that moment on, I can
barely hit the ball, except in short chips or putts. My tee-offs and fairway shots

are pathetic. Off-the-scale pathetic. I try everything: teeing up high, teeing up low. Woods, irons. Teeing up on the fairway. Little backswing. Big backswing. Hitting the ball hard. Nice, easy, slow swing. Nothing works. I top the ball with almost every topping nuance ever written or talked about: skidding off the top, just below the curve, straight right, six inches ahead, bumping along the ground, straight up in the air. And I whiff. I whiff big-time.

All of which is humiliating, as thousands before me have been humiliated on the golf course. Except that it isn't. It's a much more subtle form of self-flagellation. Because my teammates are the most beneficent, understanding, sensitive folks imaginable, offering sympathy where appropriate; silence or feigned ignorance of the horror I have just visited upon the ball where propitious; the odd mild suggestion about what I might try next. Every once in a while I turn questioningly to Sandra and ask if I could, should, do it again. Every once in a while she says yes – but not often. Sandra is a stickler for rules, she hates a slow game, and she senses, correctly, that there is no need to inflict more self-punishment than is required of me. Another try may well mean another flub and a continued downward spiral of my confidence.

I get mad, I despair, but mainly blind fatalism takes over. I try to focus on watching my teammates. There is much to observe. Harold hits the ball better than I probably ever will. But he has a swing that would make any purist weep. He stands up to the ball in a standard fashion, swings in a manner that looks normal to me, and then, once he's hit the ball and it soars off into the stratosphere, he falls backwards and does a half-pirouette with both feet. I am at a loss for something to compare this to. The only thing that comes to mind is the mating dance of the blue-footed booby, a bird native to the Galápagos Islands. People travel halfway round the world to witness blue-footed boobies perform their mating dance. And Harold's post-swing pirouette is every bit as riveting.

Sandra's basic tee-off shot is no surprise to me. It simply soars. But Rob's, our fourth, is a revelation. His, too, simply soars, and it goes dead straight. He and Sandra vie with each other throughout the round for the most precisely placed shot. It is exhilarating to behold this little sparring match. And, as the tournament continues, Sandra warms to this competition. For the first few holes she just lets her shots fly Laura Davies–style, ever so slightly carelessly. But as she senses a

SANDRA REMEMBERS ANOTHER TOURNAMENT

In June 1968, two weeks after my twentieth birthday and six months after I'd turned pro, I played in the LPGA championship tournament – the big one – at a wonderful golf course called Pleasant Valley in Worcester, Massachusetts. After four days, I tied with Kathy Whitworth, nine years older than I am and still the all-time greatest woman golfer (she's won a staggering eighty-eight tournaments). I was so stunned by this turn of events that I called my father in Oakville and told him to get on the next plane down because I was going to win this tournament. Now, did I believe that? I *had* to believe it! Anyway, Kathy and I played an eighteen-hole playoff for the championship and I won by seven strokes. That was *my* first big tournament.

true equal (she has never played with Rob before), she hones her swing and her stroke. Her competitive edge sharpens. She never puts on her game face – she is filled with bonhomie throughout the game – but the presence of a true competitor clearly makes everything much more fun for her. She starts challenging Rob to Loonie (one-dollar) bets. A Loonie for landing a shot closest to the hole. Her challenges become more daring. "I could faint and hit it closer to the hole than that!" she exclaims, and proceeds to putt, holing a shot from twenty-five feet. "I think I'll just chip this one in," she says another time – and does so, in a flash, from thirty-five feet.

I am in awe. "When you make a boast, you actually *do* it," I say.

"A *boast?*" Sandra replies. "A *boast*, you say? More like a threat! Or a promise."

A promise it is. I remember reading press clippings about Sandra's first big win in 1968, six months after she turned pro. She had "boasted" then that she would win it. But it wasn't a boast: it was simply a statement of intention.

Sandra was described by reporters at the time as pert, precocious, cocky, self-confident. "Ah yes, those were the days," Sandra sighs. "Speeding across the United States with my roommate, Renée Powell, the car tapedeck blaring 'Rhinestone Cowboy.' Pert, cocky, self-confident . . . did they ever call me

humble? You bet they did *not*. It was not my place to be humble! I had to believe I would succeed. I was out there, the first Canadian ever on the Tour, a rookie. I had nothing to lose and I went for it."

She was sure she was going to win the LPGA Championship playoff before she won it, and phoned her parents to say so. Even though she knew the odds were stacked against her. "Get on a plane," she said to her father. He did. She met him at the airport, got lost both ways, won the competition on five hours' sleep. It didn't faze her. She had nerves of steel. Pressure had no effect on her; she thrived on it. The press reports are filled with comments like: "I don't think this kid knows *how* to choke."

And now, almost three decades later, what a rush to see the same Sandra competing. Just for fun this time, but the challenge clearly gets her adrenalin pumping.

It's a long course, as Sandra said, and as the afternoon wears on, the heat wilts us. David and Rob walk most of the course; on the last few holes David is clearly whacked. We experience some bizarre moments. Early in the game, Harold drives and discovers his clubhead has gone farther than his ball. And it's not just any clubhead: it's a twenty-year-old Ben Hogan. The five of us literally beat the bushes where the clubhead appears to have flown. No luck. It's gone.

I don't offer to share the driving with Sandra in our cart because she operates it like a natural extension of her body, the way an expert snorkeller is propelled by fins. She knows every square millimetre, every hole, at Lionhead with the same certainty I know my way round my desk. She speeds along pathway and over fairway like a Jet-Ski skimming Georgian Bay, leaning over the side from time to time to deftly scoop up balls without taking her foot off the accelerator.

The rules of the scramble decree that two of my drives must be used. As we approach the last holes, the pressure builds as it becomes abundantly clear that finding a useable drive of mine is going to be . . . tricky at best. But despite

Sandra's competitiveness – and she does want our team to do well in the tournament – she never puts pressure on me. Even more remarkable, she never gives up hope for my long-term golf future. This becomes evident late in the afternoon when we're all becoming a tad punchy. As I continue to hit humiliating shots, Sandra suddenly, out of nowhere, says cheerily, "You know, I've been thinking . . . this book we're going to write might just be the first of a series. You see, women out there are going to be interested in what happens to you next. You're going to go on golfing trips, and you're going to play at different places, and you're going to take a few more lessons somewhere down the line, and you're going to try out new equipment, and you're going to go through all sorts of other things."

I'm out of breath just listening.

She continues. "And someday you're going to break a hundred!"

"This is going to be a *much* better version of *Tin Cup*," Harold interjects.

"Yes! The movie!!" Sandra crows.

"Where's Kevin Costner when we need him?" I wail.

We fantasize about who will play whom. Sandra wants Glenn Close to play her. I want Michelle Pfeiffer to play me. Then I get slightly more realistic and go for Susan Sarandon. "Thelma and Louise go golfing! That leaves Geena Davis to play *you*, Sandra."

"Ohhh, she's too tall!" says Sandra.

"Who cares about verisimilitude?" say I.

Who else could embark on a fantasy trip like this when someone else's game is imploding at the rate mine is? Sandra is the eternal optimist. The eternal believer. And she trusts in people. These are marvellously endearing traits.

At last we ride into the clubhouse, weary conquerors. "You endured, my lovely," David says, giving me a hug. "No one could ask for more." Our team score is 66, six strokes under par; we have come third.

At dinner, Sandra tells our table how she wants the whole world – of women, that is – to play golf. The Way, the Truth, and the Life of Golf is real for Sandra. Anyone who takes up golf, the game of a lifetime, will be transformed by it; their life will be changed forever, for the better and for the best. These are Sandra's fervent beliefs. Sandra is the ultimate golf apostle.

And her particular mission is to women. Rob tells a charming story about his eighteen-month-old son, who can't even talk yet but can hold and swing a club in precisely the right manner. Sandra replies, "I'm not interested in your son. He'll play anyway. Tell me about your daughters!" Earlier this afternoon, she makes an indifferent shot and turns to David with: "I hit that one like a little old man, didn't I?" As David fumbles for a response, she interrupts him, "*Usually* when a man hits a shot like that they say, 'Okay, Alice. Shape up.' Or, 'You hit that one like a little old lady.'"

When I get home I call my friends Minette and Peter, because I promised I would report in after the tournament, no matter how late it was. Minette, my longtime friend, is asleep, so I tell the entire tale to Peter. We're on the phone for about half an hour and we have one of the best, fullest conversations we've ever had. Peter and I have known each other since he and Minette married, two years ago. We've liked each other instinctively since we met, but we only see each other through flashes of lightning, usually at hectic social gatherings.

And now this conversation, conducted through the metaphor of golf, tells me more about Peter than anything we've ever talked about. One more example of the cliché about learning all you need to know about a person through a game of golf. We talk about honesty, because someone he golfs with is not honest about scoring. We talk about the drawbacks of over-competitiveness and the pluses of taking the game seriously enough to make it a challenge. We talk about positivism and negativism. Peter says he only wants to hear the positives about the tournament. I get to the negatives soon enough, and he makes it his business to console me. "Oh, we all go through that stage [my non-stop topping of the ball] when we're beginners at golf," he says with a comforting air of dismissiveness. We talk about Lionhead, a course he recently played and enjoyed hugely. We laugh a lot. As I hang up, I feel bonded with Peter in a way I have not been before. Golf is the vehicle. He is concerned about how I did; and he's interested in the details of the game. What more could one ask of a friend?

CHAPTER 18

THE 19TH HOLE

I survived the tournament, but only just. I am convinced it was the worst round of golf I've ever played, the worst of my grand (to date) total of thirteen rounds. I still believe this. But I also learned something important, to wit: nobody really cares how you hit the ball; only you do. So shut up about it.

David gave me high praise in this regard the day after the tournament. He said he thought I had behaved admirably, given the extent of my implosion. "Dottie Pepper would have thrown tantrums," he said, referring to the appropriately named American pro.

"Well," I reply, "I'm hardly in her league."

"Doesn't matter," he says. "There's *nothing* more tedious than playing with someone who isn't playing well and goes on and on about what happened and why, berating themselves. You behaved with admirable restraint."

I also learned that golf feeds on negative memory banks. David carried a mini tape recorder round the course. As I listen to his tape, I discover that I've completely erased several good shots from my memory of the tournament. Why? Because I got progressively worse and because my concentration evaporated after the first nine holes. David's concentration also lagged; he accidentally left the tape on pause during seven holes! Maybe just as well. But on the eleven holes he recorded intact, I made eleven, count 'em, good shots: four drives, four putts, one pitch, one chip, and one fairway shot. (He had some rich descriptions of some of my other shots, namely: "alas, one averts one's gaze," and "one of Loral's 'top jobs' – north, northeast, about fifteen yards.")

Six of my shots were used in the final totting up – two drives (obligatory) plus four putts (*not* obligatory). Six shots out of our team total of 66. The hard, cold numbers make my contribution look almost respectable. And David records at least one "sensational putt." Plus Sandra commented favourably on my chipping and pitching, which she said were competently done, without the identifying stigmata of the beginner.

So, after three months, half my game, my short game, is perfectly respectable.

This leaves my long game, which, my rationalizations above notwithstanding, is woeful. For the moment. And no matter how brilliant your short game is, it is impossible to play the game with a smile on your lips and a song in your heart if you are not reasonably confident that you will hit the ball into the air a decent distance off the tee. Ask Jim Ritts. Until I get that back, I will continue to beat myself up. And try to shut up about it.

My proudest achievement from the tournament: Somewhere along the way, Sandra told David that I have a real feel for the game. I know this is true, because the tape doesn't lie! I quote: "Loral has a real feel for the game. She doesn't waste time, she knows what she has to do. She just gets on with it."

Thank you, Sandra. I humbly (sorry!) accept this accolade. Humbly and proudly.

Yes, I instinctively hate slow golf. I hate losing the rhythm, the momentum. And I'm pretty good about blanking out the past shot and getting on with the game "on a going-forward basis," my stepson's hip phrase for negotiating deals. Since golf is about focusing on the moment, the present moment, one shot at a time, I must be on the right track. Just get on with it.

The tournament taught me, too, that corporate golf is not my bag (although I did enjoy the scramble format: it's a great way to get through eighteen holes and to enjoy three other people's company). But I can do without the corporate culture: big signs advertising sponsors, shiny new cars to be won on a couple of holes. (I was stunned to learn that if you actually *win* one, you lose your amateur status – for accepting a prize worth more than $750. It's a rich thought: Loral takes up golf at age fifty-three; plays in a tournament three months later; wins a car . . . and loses her amateur status. Loral a pro, after three months of golf!)

I don't win the car, so the question of my status does not arise. I win two other things, however. For coming third, the four of us win golf bags big enough to camp out in – with a beer ad down one side of each. Not Henry Longhurst-friendly bags, but David has his eye on mine. And I win a six-foot submarine party sandwich! (Appropriately, my dinner prize.)

But I dislike electric carts and big corporate courses. The *raison d'être* for Ontario's finest public golf course seems to be large corporate outings. And in the dog days of summer, beleaguered Lionhead tells the tale. The putting greens, an insipid, pale green, neither look nor feel like real grass, and they are *awash* with spike marks. Give me Oakville Executive's greens at sundown, glistening with dew. Or Parry Sound's damp, rich forest greens at dawn.

Yes, scrap the banquets, scrap the speeches, scrap the prizes. I can do without all that. I just wanna play golf. Quietly. Into the sunset. With good friends. Or alone.

GLOSSARY

(Illustrations by Andy Donato)

ADDRESS: As in, "Address the ball." This is your starting position. It includes golf's Four Basics: **grip**, **stance**, **posture**, and **alignment**.

ALBATROSS: Also **double eagle**. Three strokes under **par**. That is, holing the ball in two shots on a par-5 hole. On a par-4 hole, an albatross would be called a hole in one.

ALIGNMENT: Lining up your **clubface** to your **target**. (Your body is parallel to, but *left* of, the target.)

ALL SQUARE: All players are even in **match play**.

APPROACH SHOT: A **fairway** shot intended to "approach" (get close to) the **pin**.

APRON: Also **fringe**. *See* **fringe**.

AWAY: Farthest from the hole. As in, "You're away." (Or, the saddest words in golf, "You're *still* away.") The person who is away hits the ball first.

BACK NINE: *See* **front nine**.

BACKSWING: The first part of the full golf swing, when the club is taken back from the ball to the point where it starts back down again.

BACK TEE: Also **championship tee**. *See* **forward tee**.

BALL MARK: Also **pitch mark** or **divot mark**. A mark (a slight depression) made by a ball landing on the **green**. You repair this ball mark using either a divot repairer (a tool you can buy in any golf shop) or a **tee**.

BALL MARKER: A flat, round, tacked disk the size of a small coin, used to mark the ball's position on the **green** so that another player may **putt**.

BIRDIE: A score of one under **par** for the hole. You "get a birdie" or "go for birdie." On a par-5 hole you hole the ball in four strokes; on a par-4, in three; on a par-3, in two.

BITE: As in the cry, "*Bite!*" meaning "May the ball land and 'bite' the **green**" – stay in one place without rolling.

BLADE PUTTER: A **putter** with a very narrow clubhead, the same on each side. You can putt right- or left-handed with a blade putter.

BOGEY: A score of one over **par** for the hole. On a par-5, you hole the ball in six strokes; on a par-4, in five; on a par-3, in four.

BREAK, BREAKS: The direction a **putt** rolls on the **green**. The ball will break depending on the slope of the green. The break of the green determines where you aim your putt.

BREAKING 100: Scoring less than 100 strokes during a **round** of golf. A common goal for **club golfers**.

BUNKER: *See* **sand bunker**.

CADDY: A person paid to carry a golfer's bag. Traditionally, caddies know the golf course well and give advice to the golfer.

CARRY: The distance a ball travels through the air.

CHAMPIONSHIP TEE: Also **back tee**. *See* **forward tee**.

CHIP, CHIPPING: A short **lofted** shot from around the **green**.

CHIP-AND-RUN SHOT: Also pitch-and-run. A common term in the **short game**, in which you hit (chip) the ball a short distance and let it roll (run) on the **green** towards the **hole**.

CLOSED CLUBFACE: The **clubface** is angled to the left of the **target**.

CLOSED STANCE: In the **address** position, the right (back) foot is pulled back from the ball, and from a line that is perpendicular to the **target** line. Note that, in golf, the "back" foot refers to the foot farthest from the target.

CLUBFACE: The flat front of the golf club, with which you hit the ball. In the centre of the clubface is the **sweet spot**.

CLUB GOLFER: Term used to describe the average amateur golfer (in contrast to the **pro** or **professional golfer**).

CLUBHEAD: The entire head of the golf club.

CLUBHEAD SPEED: The speed with which the **clubhead** hits the ball.

COLLAR: Also **apron, first cut, fringe, skirt.** *See* **fringe.**

CUP: *See* **hole.**

DIMPLES: The round indentations on a golf ball.

DIVOT: You often "take a divot" (a piece of turf) when you hit the golf ball. You try to hit the ball before you take a divot.

DIVOT MARK: Also **ball mark** or **pitch mark.** *See* **ball mark.**

DOGLEG: When the **fairway** bends left or right on its way to the green. As in, "dogleg left" or "dogleg right."

DOUBLE EAGLE: *See* **albatross.**

DRIVE: A tee-off shot. The drive is the first shot on each hole. To drive the ball you "tee up" your ball on a **tee.**

DRIVER: The longest, least **lofted** club (excluding the **putter**) in the golf bag (sometimes marked with the number "1"), used to **tee off** with on a long hole. A driver is always a **wood** (although today, woods are usually made of metal) and is designed to achieve maximum power and distance. New golfers often use a 3-wood instead of a driver because it's a bit shorter and easier to handle.

DRIVING RANGE: Also **practice range.** An area intended for practising the **long game.** Usually a large field, with distances of 100 to 200 or 250 yards marked with flags, fronted by a long line of **practice tees.** At a commercial driving range you "buy" (rent, effectively) a metal bucket containing forty to one hundred balls.

DROP: You "drop" the ball or "take" a drop. To drop the ball, stand straight with your arm parallel to the ground at shoulder level and be sure to drop the ball no closer to the hole than you already are. There are free drops and drops where you incur a penalty.

EAGLE: A score of two strokes under **par** on a **hole**. An **eagle** on a par-5 hole would be three; on a par-4, two. On a par-3, an eagle would be called a hole in one.

EXECUTIVE COURSE: A short golf course, composed of mainly (sometimes all) par-3 holes. It has nothing to do with business, as the name might imply.

FADE: *See* How Will You Hit the Ball?

FAIRWAY: The mown, grassed playing area of a golf course, between the **tee** and the **green**.

FAIRWAY WOODS: **Woods** normally used to hit long shots from the **fairway**. These include the 2-, 3-, 4-, 5-, 7-, 9-,and 11-woods. The 7-and the 9-wood have become very popular recently, particularly among women, because they're long and **lofted** and easier to hit with than their **iron** counterparts, the 3- and the 4-iron.

FIRST CUT: Also **apron, collar, fringe, skirt**. *See* **fringe**.

FLAG, FLAGSTICK: The flag on a stick that shows the position of each of the holes on a golf course.

FLANGE: The wide, heavy bottom of a **sand wedge**.

FLANGE PUTTER: A currently popular **putter** with a wide, flat bottom.

FLEX: The amount of bend or movement of a golf-club's **shaft**. The flex varies from club to club. In general, the stronger you are, the less flex you require. So women usually are comfortable with more flexible shafts than are men.

FOLLOW-THROUGH: The finishing part of the full golf swing, after hitting the ball. In the follow-through position, the player faces the **target** and finishes in balance.

FORE: The traditional danger cry in golf. If you hit a ball near another person, you should call *"Fore!"* to alert him or her.

FORWARD TEE: Golf courses usually have two or three tees to accommodate different levels of players. The front tee is called the forward tee, or the **ladies' tee**. The **middle tee** is called the **men's tee**. And the **back tee** is called the **championship tee** or **professional tee**. The neutral terms forward, middle, and back tee reflect the realities of golf today. Play the tee that matches your playing ability.

FRIED EGG: A ball half-buried in sand.

FRINGE: Also **apron**, **collar**, **first cut**, **skirt**. The closely cut grass (more so than the **fairway**, less so than the **green**) bordering the green.

FRONT NINE, BACK NINE: Every golf course is laid out in groups of nine holes, and a full **round** of golf includes eighteen holes. The first nine holes played are called the **front nine**; the second nine holes played are called the **back nine**.

GOLF BAG: The bag in which you carry your golf clubs and other paraphernalia needed on the golf course (balls, tees, towel, drink, snack, sunscreen, golf umbrella, rainjacket, etc.).

GOLF GLOVE: A single glove, made of leather or a synthetic, used to help the player grip the club. A right-handed golfer wears a glove on the left hand; a left-handed golfer on the right.

GOLF PRO: A professional golfer who earns a living by playing or teaching golf.

GOLF SHOES: Sturdy, flat-heeled shoes, usually with leather uppers, with heavily ribbed soles or **spikes** to help the golfer stay grounded when hitting a shot. ("Soft" spikes are increasingly popular today because they do less damage to the greens than the traditional harder, longer spikes.)

GOLF SHOP: *See* **pro shop**.

GOLF TOURNAMENT: A competitive **round** of golf and related social events for a large or small group, organized by a golf club, corporation, charity, or other group to raise money, have fun, or encourage good business relations. Golf tournaments usually include food, drink, prizes, and socializing.

GOLF UMBRELLA: A large umbrella that covers you *and* your golf bag if you're caught in rain on the golf course.

GRAIN: The direction in which the grass on a **putting green** is growing. When you **read a green**, you look closely at the grain of the grass and then putt "with the grain" (faster) or "against the grain" (slower).

GREEN: Short for the **putting green**. The closely mowed, manicured area surrounding the **hole** or **cup** where only **putting** is allowed.

GREEN IN REGULATION: To "reach the green in regulation," you must advance from **tee off** to **green** within **par**, allowing for two putts on the green. So, on a par-5, you reach the green in regulation with three shots; on par-4, with two shots, and on a par-3 in one. This allows two putts for par.

GREENS FEE: The cost of a **round** of golf. You pay for a round of golf in the **pro shop**. The price includes a small pencil and **scorecard**. (Golf carts and pullcarts usually are paid for separately from the greens fee.)

GRIP: The rubber or leather part of the upper part of the golf shaft that you hold onto, *plus* the position of your hands when you hold on to a golf club. There are three standard grips: the Baseball (or Ten-Finger) Grip, the Overlapping (or Vardon) Grip, and the Interlocking Grip.

GROOVES: The parallel lines on the **clubface**, which help put spin on the ball.

HANDICAP: The handicap system enables golfers of different abilities to play a competitive round of golf together and compete on an even footing.

HAZARD: Any permanent obstacle on a course, such as a river, lake, or bunker.

HEADCOVER: A soft, socklike cover to protect **clubheads** (particularly **woods** and **putters**) from marking.

HEADS UP: The expression used by a golfer about to hit a ball, to alert playing partners who have strayed ahead.

HEEL: The back part of the **clubhead** where the **hosel** meets it.

HOLE: Also **cup**. The final destination for the golf ball; you must "hole" the ball eighteen times over a **round** of golf. The four-and-a-quarter-inch hole is moved around each **green** every day to vary the game and to even out wear and tear on the green.

HOLE OUT: **Putting** into the **hole** on the **green**.

HONOUR: The first person to tee off has the "honour." The person with the lowest score on the previous hole wins the honour on the next tee.

HOOK: *See* How Will You Hit the Ball?

HOSEL: The neck of the golf club just above the **clubhead** where it meets the **shaft**.

IMPACT: The moment the **clubhead** meets the ball.

IRON: "Iron" (now steel) golf clubs with thin, knifelike **clubheads** numbered 1 through 9. They're used more for accuracy than distance (**woods** are used more for distance than accuracy).

LADIES' TEE: *See* **forward tee**.

LATERAL WATER HAZARD: A **water hazard** beside the **fairway**.

LIE, LIES: The position in which the golf ball comes to rest and "lies" on the ground. There are uphill, downhill, and sidehill lies, as well as endless other variations on the way the ball nestles in or on top of grass or sand. There is also the unplayable lie, which you cannot play, period (the classic one being between a rock and a hard place). You take a **penalty** and a **drop**, and play on.

LINE OF A PUTT: The line of a putt is the line you intend the ball to follow into the **hole** when you **putt**. Golf etiquette decrees that you do not step on a golf partner's **putting line**, because in doing so you may subtly alter it.

LINKS: A seaside golf course, typically rugged, with dunes, coarse grass, and uneven terrain. The traditional links course in Scotland is laid out parallel to the shoreline, with the **front nine** holes extending away from the clubhouse and the **back nine** coming back towards it.

LOFT: The angle on the **clubface**. The greater the loft of the **clubface**, the higher the ball will travel and the shorter the distance.

LONG GAME: The part of the golf game that requires the full golf swing. This includes **teeing-off** and **fairway** shots. Although less than half the game involves the full swing, the average **club golfer** spends much more time honing her **full swing** than she does her **short game**.

LONG IRONS: The irons with the longest **shafts** and the least **loft**. Technically, long irons include 1-, 2-, 3-irons, but women usually don't use 1- and 2-irons. So long irons for women are 3- and 4-irons.

LPGA: Ladies Professional Golf Association.

MALLET PUTTER: A style of **putter** shaped like a mallet or half-moon, crescent-shaped on one side and flat on the other.

MATCH PLAY: Familiarly called **hole play**. A **round** of golf in which score is kept between competitors hole by hole instead of stroke by stroke.

MEDAL PLAY: *See* **stroke play**.

MEN'S TEE: Now **middle tee**. *See* **forward tee**.

MID-IRONS, MIDDLE IRONS: The mid-sized **irons**, with medium lengths and **lofts**. For women, the 6- and 7-irons are mid-irons.

MIDDLE TEE: Formerly **men's tee**: *See* **forward tee**.

MULLIGAN: A shot that you neglect to count in your score. Players frequently "take a mulligan" when they hit a bad **tee** shot. In a friendly **round**, you state how many mulligans you plan to take *before* you begin playing.

NET SCORE: A player's score for a **round** after her **handicap** has been deducted.

OFF THE PACE: An expression used in professional golf tournaments that means the player is falling behind. A player who is "two strokes off the pace" is two strokes behind the leader.

OPEN CLUBFACE: The **clubface** is angled to the right of the **target**.

OPEN STANCE: In the **address** position, the left (front) foot is pulled back from the ball, and from a line that is perpendicular to the **target** line. Note that, in golf, "front" foot refers to the foot closest to the target.

OUT OF BOUNDS: Area outside the playing area of a golf course, marked by white out-of-bounds stakes. When you hit a ball out of bounds, the **penalty** is **stroke plus distance**.

PAR: The optimum number of **strokes** or shots required from **tee-off** to **hole out** on each hole, and for each nine and eighteen holes. Minimum par per hole is 3 (as in par 3); maximum is 5 (as in par 5). The average par for eighteen holes is 72.

PENALTY: Penalties in **stroke play** are measured in **strokes** added to the score.

PGA: Professional Golfers Association.

PIN: *See* **flag, flagstick**.

PIN HIGH: Hitting a ball pin high means hitting it as far as the flag, in line with it on the **green**.

PIN PLACEMENT: The position, or placement, of the **pin**, or **flag**, on the **green**. The pin is changed daily on each green.

PITCH, PITCHING: A **lofted** shot near the **green**. Approximately 75 per cent of the distance a pitched ball travels is through the air, 25 per cent along the ground.

PITCH MARK: Also **ball mark** or **divot mark**. *See* **ball mark**.

PITCHING WEDGE: A short **lofted** iron, used for **pitching** the ball.

PIVOT: The turn or twist your body makes in the **backswing** and forward swing.

PLANE: The path or arc of a golf swing.

PLAYING THROUGH: Golf etiquette suggests that, if you are holding up players behind you, you allow them to play through (go ahead of you).

POSTURE: How you hold your body when you **address** the ball. One of the Four Basics of Golf.

PRACTICE PUTTING GREEN: A putting green at a **driving range** or golf club intended for practising putting. A practice putting green has several **holes** marked by **flags** so that players can practise different distances, angles, and slopes, and get a feel for the speed of the **greens**.

PRACTICE RANGE: *See* **driving range**.

PRACTICE TEE: A **teeing-off** pad (grass or artificial turf) on a **driving range** or **practice range**.

PRO SHOP: A combination office and store at a golf club or golf course. The person behind the cash register will take your **greens fee**, tell you when your **tee-off time** is, discuss club protocol and scheduling, arrange lessons with the club **pro**, etc. He or she will also help you with purchases in the store, which sells golf equipment and clothing.

PROFESSIONAL TEE: *See* **forward tee**.

PULL: *See* How Will You Hit the Ball?

PULLCART: A two-wheeled cart (which you rent or buy) designed to hold a golf bag, which the player pulls around the golf course.

PUSH: *See* How Will You Hit the Ball?

PUTT, PUTTING: On the **green**, you **stroke** the ball towards the **hole** with a golf club known as a **putter**.

PUTTER: A golf club with a flat **clubface** and little **loft**, used for **stroking** the ball towards the **hole** on a putting green. Putters come in several shapes, the most common of which are the **blade putter**, the **flange putter**, and the **mallet putter**.

PUTTING GREEN: *See* **green**.

READING THE GREEN: Reading the green is deciding ("reading") which way the ball is going to roll after you have stroked it. To read a green you observe the slope of the green (to decide how the ball will **break**) as well as the **grain**, type, length, and moisture content of the grass.

RED STAKES: Red stakes mark a **lateral water hazard**. If you cannot play the ball from within the red stakes, you must take a one-shot penalty.

RELEASE: You release the club during the golf swing when the wrists go from a cocked to uncocked position, creating maximum **clubhead speed** at **impact**.

ROUND: A round of golf means eighteen **holes**, a complete game. You "play a round of golf."

ROUGH: Longer grass bordering **fairways** and **greens**. Referred to as "the rough" or "in the rough."

RUB OF THE GREEN: An unlucky shot that just happens (not to be confused with a bad shot). "Oh, that's the rub of the green" means "That's just the way it is – there's nothing you can do about it." *Example:* You hit what starts out as a great shot, but it hits a sprinkler head in front of the **green** and ricochets into a **sand bunker**.

SAND BUNKER: Also **sand trap**. A depression filled with sand is considered a **hazard**. The number of bunkers on a golf course is arbitrary: there is no maximum or minimum. Golfers try to avoid hitting shots into **sand bunkers**, because they are tricky to get out of. There are special rules governing **sand play**, but you do not incur a **penalty** simply by hitting a ball into a bunker.

SAND PLAY: When you accidentally hit a ball into a **sand bunker** (or **sand trap**), hitting the ball out of the bunker is referred to as sand play.

SAND TRAP: *See* **sand bunker**.

SAND WEDGE: A **lofted** iron with a wide **flange** with added weight, designed for **sand play**.

SCORECARD: When you pay your **greens fee** you are given a **scorecard**, with columns in which to enter your and your partners' scores. The local rules are printed on the back.

SCRAMBLE: A golf game usually played in a **golf tournament**, in which teams of four players follow the best ball hit on every shot. This encourages all levels of golfers to participate.

SCRATCH PLAYER: An experienced golf player with a zero **handicap**, who normally plays a **par** game or better.

SET OF CLUBS: A full set of clubs includes fourteen clubs. The usual mix is six to eight irons (short, mid-, long), a driver, two to four fairway woods, a pitching wedge, a sand wedge, and a putter. The rules of golf limit golfers to a maximum of fourteen clubs in their golf bag. There is no minimum number of clubs.

SHAFT: The rod of the golf club between the **grip** and the **clubhead**, made of steel or graphite. The shaft is the only part of the club that moves.

SHANK: *See* How Will You Hit the Ball?

SHORT GAME: The short game refers to all the shots you make around the green. It comprises **putting**, **chipping**, **pitching**, and **sand play**.

SHORT IRONS: The 8- and 9-iron, which are the shorter, more **lofted**, **irons** in your golf bag.

SIT! SIT DOWN!: Expression used by golfers when they want their shot to land on the green without rolling. *See* **bite**.

SKIRT: *See* **fringe**.

SLICE: *See* How Will You Hit the Ball?

SOLE: The bottom of a golf club.

SPIKES: The studs in the soles of **golf shoes** that help the golfer stay grounded when hitting the ball and that grip the ground when the golfer is swinging the club on difficult **lies**.

SQUARE: The position of the **clubface** or feet when they are at right angles to the target.

STANCE: The way you stand (feet shoulder-width in a balanced position) when you **address** the ball. One of the Four Basics of Golf.

STROKE: The term used during **putting** (instead of hitting the ball, you **stroke** it); also the term for the number of times you hit the ball during a **round** of golf.

STROKE PLAY: Also **medal play**. A **round** of golf in which you count every stroke. The fewest strokes determine the winner. *See* **match play**.

STROKE PLUS DISTANCE: A two-stroke **out-of-bounds** penalty. You add two strokes to your score. One is a penalty stroke; the other is added by hitting a ball for a second time from the same place (thus subtracting the distance you've already hit the ball).

SWEET SPOT: The spot in the middle of the **clubface**, which produces perfect contact when you hit it. The **sweet spot** on some golf clubs is marked.

TAKEAWAY: The beginning of the **backswing**, when you take your club away from the ball at **address**.

TARGET: The place you aim your ball towards. This can be the **flag** or **pin** (the **hole**) or it can be somewhere closer to where you are on the **fairway** or **green**.

TEE: A wood or plastic peg used to elevate the ball before **teeing off** on a flat area allocated for this purpose, and *also* called a **tee** or **teeing ground**.

TEEING GROUND: *See* **tee.**

TEE MARKER: Golfers tee off inside two colour-coded tee markers on the **tee.** Most golf courses have three sets of tees – **forward, middle,** and **back; forward tees** are red, **middle** are white, and **back** are blue.

TEE-OFF: The first shot of each **hole** is called your tee shot.

TEE-OFF TIME: The time you book (usually by telephone) with the **pro shop** for **teeing off** at your first **hole.**

TEMPO: The pace or speed of your golf swing. It should be balanced: neither too fast nor too slow. Tempo, rhythm, and timing of your swing and your game are related concepts.

TOE: The front end of the **clubhead.**

TOURNAMENT: *See* **golf tournament.**

TURN, THE: The transition between the **front** and the **back nine holes** of a **round** of golf. The turn also refers to the body's **pivot** during the golf swing.

WAGGLE: When you **address** the ball, you waggle (swing the clubhead to and fro over the ball) in order to settle into a relaxed position before making your swing. Your waggle establishes the **tempo** for your shot and helps keep your hands, fore-arms, and shoulders relaxed.

WATER HAZARD: Any body of water on or adjacent to (*see* **lateral water hazard**) a golf course. It is considered a **hazard,** because you must avoid it in order to keep the ball in play. If you hit the ball *into* the water hazard, you incur a one-**stroke** penalty.

WEDGE: *See* **pitching wedge, sand wedge.** A **lofted** iron. Wedge refers to the shape of the **clubhead.**

WHIFF: The golfer's term for missing a ball completely. Usually involves a mighty swing in the direction of the ball, and ends with a sound of metal slicing through air or earth. A whiff counts as a **stroke.**

WHITE STAKES: White stakes mark an area that is **out of bounds**.

WOOD, WOODS: A type of club used for long-range shots. The **clubhead**, much larger than the **clubhead** of an **iron**, originally was made of wood; nowadays it usually is metal.

WORM-BURNER: Slang expression for badly hit ball that doesn't go far and hugs the ground.

WRISTCOCK: During the full golf swing, the wrists hinge in a wristcock during the **backswing** and unhinge on the downswing.

GLOSSARY ADDENDUM

HOW WILL YOU HIT THE BALL? LET US COUNT THE WAYS

When you're a new golfer, making contact with the ball is a triumph. Anything in the *air* with a little distance added is a victory. But the infinite number and the uncountable variations of horrible things you will manage to do to the ball will amaze you. These are shots you will want to forget immediately. But, like it or not, other people will label them. So you might as well get to know what they mean. Here are some of them:

FAT: A fat shot is just what it implies; you take a lot of earth; you hit the ground before you hit the ball. The result? It doesn't go far because hitting into the ground slows the **clubhead** down.

THIN: Conversely, hitting the ball thin means you hit too high on the ball. When you hit the ball thin, you've caught the ball on the upsweep and usually the shot goes straight, low, and short. Very thin, you've topped it.

THICK: There's no such shot! (*See* Chapter 9.)

LEFT TO RIGHT SHOTS

FADE: A fade starts out more or less straight and then falls gradually, or fades, to the right (or left, for the left-hander). As the word implies, this is not a dramatic move to the right, like a **slice.**

PUSH: A straight ball that goes right of the **target.** The opposite of a **pull.**

SHANK: A shank is the s-word in golf. No one wants to say the word "shank," because the ball travels at right angles to you. Also called a lateral.

SLICE: Like a **fade,** a **slice** starts out more or less straight. But then it makes a dramatic right turn.

RIGHT TO LEFT SHOTS

DRAW: A draw is the mirror-image of a **fade.** A draw starts out more or less straight and then moves very gradually to the left (or right, for the left-hander).

HOOK: A hook is a mirror-image image of a **slice.** It starts out more or less straight, then makes a dramatic left turn.

PULL: A straight ball that goes left of the target. The opposite of a **push.**

ETC., ETC. SHOTS

SKY, SKYING: As in, "I skyed it." A skyed ball goes straight up, very high – and then straight down.

SPRAY, SPRAYING: Again, just what it sounds like. Your first shot goes way to the right (or left). Your next shot goes way to the left (or right). Your next shot goes . . . wherever. You spray the ball all over the place with no rhyme or reason to it all. You have no control of the ball. Time to go back to the **practice range.**

TOP, TOPPING (Loral's Specialty Shot): You catch the top of the ball – the very top – with the bottom of the golf club – the very bottom. Result? The ball rolls along the ground.

INDEX

Page numbers in **boldface** indicate illustrations.